God Is at Work in You

A Practical Guide
to Growth in the Spirit

Ralph Rath

Greenlawn Press

ISBN 0-937779-11-3
Library of Congress Catalog Card Number: 89-83731

Greenlawn Press
107 South Greenlawn
South Bend, IN 46617

Cover design by Cae Carnick.
Cover photo copyright by Jean-Claude Lejeune.

CONTENTS

Preface   iv

Introduction   v

Section One: Spiritual Growth

Chapter One: Prayer   1

Chapter Two: Reading Scripture   10

Chapter Three: The Lord's Guidance   18

Section Two: Overcoming Sin

Chapter Four: The World   29

Chapter Five: The Flesh   38

Chapter Six: The Devil   47

Chapter Seven: Repentance   60

Section Three: Reaching Out

Chapter Eight: Evangelizing Others   69

Chapter Nine: Personal Testimony   81

Preface

This book is based on a series of talks developed by leaders of the People of Praise covenant community, headquartered in South Bend, Indiana. They have been given for many years to audiences primarily composed of people newly baptized in the Spirit. The talks have been very successful. Because they existed only in outline form, each speaker was expected to develop a complete talk from the outline and to add his personal examples to illustrate it. This is what I have done in writing this book. While all the basic material comes from the outlines, I have added examples from my personal experience.

—Ralph Rath

Introduction

When an individual is baptized in the Spirit, a new power is given to the person. There is a new enthusiasm for spiritual things. There is an eagerness to pray and to read Scripture. The Bible seems much more meaningful. There is a desire to share this new closeness with the Lord with friends and acquaintances.

The People of Praise, an ecumenical Christian covenant community, has long realized that it is important not only to introduce people to this new life in the Spirit, but also to encourage them to grow to spiritual maturity. A series of talks, called the Christian Living Series, was developed to assist people in the first few months of living in a new, vibrant spiritual dimension. The final talk, on discerning the Lord's will, was designed to lead the individual to make a commitment that would further encourage spiritual growth. Joining a covenant community was given as one of several possible options. Continuing to participate actively in a prayer group and increased involvement in a local church were other options.

Over the years, the talks have proven very successful. Group after group and individual after individual have expressed heartfelt gratitude for the knowledge and support the teaching series provided them.

Until this book was written, the Christian Living Series only existed in outline form. The speaker was expected to develop the outline into a complete talk, using personal examples and illustrations. The series has been revised a number of times over the years. In the latest configuration, there are nine talks (or chapters) divided into three sections.

The first section has three chapters: on prayer, on reading Scripture and on listening to the Lord for guidance. The purpose of the section is to lead the individual into forming habits of daily prayer, regular—even daily—Scripture reading, and attentiveness to God's direction.

The second section deals with the reality of sin. There are chapters on the three principal sources of temptation: the world, the flesh and the devil. The fourth chapter deals with our responsibility for our actions—our guilt—and with repentance and reconciliation.

The third section deals with effective Christian outreach. It is designed to harness the "zeal of the first hour" of the person newly baptized in the Spirit. There are two talks on sharing the Good News—one on the necessity of witnessing to others and the other on giving a personal testimony.

You can use the Scripture readings for daily prayer or you can select from them what you are most interested in learning more about. You can use the discussion questions as a guide for reflection or you can go right on to the next chapter. You're the boss.

You may be reading this by yourself. As was said, the material originally came from outlines of talks given to groups. You are perfectly free, of course, to read the material at your own pace in the solitude of your room. You can skim through or you can spend a lot of time reflecting on a particular section.

Here are some suggestions if the book is used for group discussions. Each member of the group can obtain a copy and read the material before the weekly meeting. The leader can go over the material quickly and then a good deal of time can be set aside for discussion. As another option, the leader alone may have a copy of the book. He will give the talk and then lead the discussion. Be flexible. Use this book in ways that will bring your group the most benefits.

The Scripture readings before the chapters are designed for daily prayer during the week before the discussion group meets. If each member does not have a copy of the book, a list of the various Scripture passages could be handed out ahead of time.

In those cases where each member of the group has a book, the discussion questions could be looked over ahead of time. This would provide more time for people to prepare their comments.

The primary audience for this book, as has been said, is people who have recently been baptized in the Spirit, but other Christians will benefit from the program. They should find it a tool to help them grow closer to Jesus. It may also be a great refresher course for persons who were first baptized in the Spirit years ago.

It goes without saying that this book is not meant merely to be read. It is meant to be meditated on and prayed over. It will take your dedication and prayerful enthusiasm to make these words meaningful in your life.

Section I

CHAPTER ONE: PRAYER

Daily Scripture Readings

1. Read Matthew 6:9-13. The Lord's Prayer has been called the perfect prayer. Read it over several times and meditate on each line.

2. Read Matthew 11:28-30. Jesus wants you to call on him in your troubles. He wants to comfort you. He wants to take your burdens on himself. Thank him for this loving service and then give him your burdens.

3. Read 2 Corinthians 5:6-10. Someday we will walk with Jesus in paradise. Now our contact with him is through faith. Pray that your faith may increase.

4. Read Mark 14:32-42. Consider the three apostles. At this most trying time in Jesus' life, they fall asleep. Do we persevere in prayer even when we don't feel like it?

5. Read 1 Kings 19:9-13. Where do we find God? Is it only in earthquake and fire? Or can we have a special sense of God's presence in the still, quiet time of prayer?

6. Read Matthew 7:7-11. Do we believe that God hears all our prayers? If we don't get exactly what we request, can we be confident that God is giving us something better? Is God more loving and generous than our earthly parents?

7. Read Exodus 34:29-35. Our prayer is an encounter with God. How can our acts and our words "shine" after this encounter so that people will know we have been talking with God? How will our daily prayer change our daily lives?

Prayer is essential to growth as a Christian. Sometimes it is easy. Many times it is difficult. How can we improve our prayer life?

Personal prayer is much more enjoyable for me since I have become involved in the charismatic renewal. I look forward to my morning prayer time (once I manage to get myself up and doing things). It is not a perfect prayer time, and I have many distractions, but I think it is a good prayer time.

In my youth, this was not the case. I read some spiritual books and asked for some spiritual direction and for years I tried to get in 25 minutes of mental prayer a day. It was really tough. I did not enjoy it at all. I did not look forward to it. It was hard work trying to follow the routines in the meditation books. I got very little spiritual consolation. I rarely felt close to God during my prayer times.

I also was encouraged to go on annual retreats. Some of my friends found them very helpful. They could remember talks they'd heard years before. They remembered many details of the talks on the current retreat and were able to discuss these at length during break times. The things I most recall from these retreat experiences were the times I walked along the road at night and looked at the lights of the city in the distance and counted the hours until we would get back to normal life.

On the other hand, I had many positive prayer experiences in my younger days, but these fell into certain categories. I always liked liturgical prayer. For many, many years, I went to daily Mass. I was an altar server from a very young age. (While I liked to go to Mass, I disliked many devotional events like the weekly Holy Hour at my small-town parish in Minnesota. I tried to promise my grandmother who raised me several attendances at Masses if I could skip the Holy Hour, but I was not successful in persuading her. She thought the Holy Hour also had its merits.) I was happy about brief home prayers, like the grace before meals (hunger *may* have been partly responsible for this). I was not enthusiastic about the long devotional prayers we had at home during the season of Lent.

My prayer life changed instantaneously when I was baptized in the Spirit in 1974. After hearing about the charismatic renewal for about two years, I went to my first prayer meeting and was very impressed by the rich quality of prayer there. Two months after that first prayer meeting, I was prayed with to be baptized in the Spirit and I was immediately able to participate fully in those fervent and moving prayer meetings.

My personal prayer life also changed with the baptism in the Spirit. This grace has remained with me. I now feel good when I think of spending prayer time with the Lord and when I am actually praying. Jesus is my personal friend as well as my Savior. God the Father is present when I pray. I use the gifts and the power of the Holy Spirit to overcome my weakness and distractions during prayer. Years of retreats and meditation books could not get me to like personal prayer, but baptism in the Spirit accomplished this without special effort on my part. I let the Holy Spirit change me.

I'm not trying to say that I am a statue-saint with my eyes constantly on heaven. I still have problems with distractions during prayer. I daydream. I think about what I need to do at work or around the house. Sometimes, lingering hurts or feelings of anger bother me. However, I have learned not to get upset by these things. I know I am genuinely delighted to be spending time with the Lord. As soon as I catch myself in distractions, I gently pull myself back to a prayerful attitude. I do not get upset with myself. I simply do the best I can and I know the Lord is pleased with that.

Baptism in the Holy Spirit is a powerful experience. One friend of mine received a remarkable gift of prayer through baptism in the Spirit. This individual is not well educated and he had a pretty rough life before he came to the Lord, but he was given a special gift for contemplative prayer. He regularly got up at 5 a.m. and spent two hours or more in rapt contemplation of God. As he described the experience, he did not use a book and did not say words. He just contemplated God with great joy and peace in his heart.

That's real prayer. I know I'll get that gift one day—in heaven, if not before. Until then, I'll pray the best way I can. I thank God that, because of the power of his Spirit, I now really enjoy prayer.

Prayer is contemplation of and conversation with a friend. There are difficulties, but they can be overcome.

What is prayer? It's conversation with God. It's contemplation of God. It's the way we develop our relationship with the Father, with Jesus and with the Holy Spirit.

Consider the way you relate to your best friend. You think a lot of the friend. You keep in touch by personal contact and by phone and letter. You like spending time together. You often just like doing things together.

The elements that go into making a successful human relationship are the same that go into developing a relationship with God through prayer. We need to spend time with our divine friend. We need to talk to him and be open to his talking to us. We need to learn more about our friend through reading Scripture and spiritual books. We need to lead lives that will keep us pleasing to our friend.

That sounds very simple and easy, doesn't it? Yet we all know that prayer can be difficult. Sometimes the problem involves a basic misconception of what prayer is. Consider the following bits of conversation.

"Everything I do is prayer." Sure it is! Great saints can say this and prove it by their evident holiness of life. Most people making this statement are only fooling themselves and usually fall short of the heights of sanctity.

"I can only relate to formal prayer." Many people think they need to rely on a prayer book or a rosary in order to pray. These things can be helpful at times, but we don't relate to friends only with set speeches. We need to be spontaneous in our prayer, too. The baptism in the Holy Spirit can free us to pray spontaneously.

"God doesn't work like that. He's too great to pay attention to me." It is hard to believe that the almighty, all-powerful God loves each one of us as a personal friend. Once again, only the power of the Holy Spirit can help us realize this.

Here is another objection to prayer.

"I don't believe I am really called to a regular prayer life." This could be a real predicament. If you pray consistently, you will realize you *are* called to a regular prayer life, but how do you motivate yourself to get started? Read the Scriptures. Read devotional books. Talk to people who pray regularly. Attend prayer meetings and church services. Keep working at it. God will bless you. Be sure to seek baptism in the Spirit, if you have not yet experienced this grace.

> Come to me, all who labor and are heavy laden, and I
> will give you rest. Take my yoke upon you, and learn
> from me (Mt. 11:28-29).

Act according to what you know to be true, not the way things seem at the moment or according to the way you feel.

Walk by faith, not by sight (2 Cor. 5:7).

"My life is so disorganized." Well, get organized. Set priorities and make prayer a top priority. Schedule a prayer period in prime time. Get a good alarm clock, if necessary. Select a good time to pray and a good place to pray.

"I have serious sin in my life." Repent. Receive forgiveness from the Lord. Stop sinning. Realize that repentant sinners can have an especially rich prayer life. They have much to be thankful for.

"I don't know how to pray." Read books on prayer. Attend workshops on prayer. Talk to people who pray regularly. Try various methods of prayer and adopt one that works for you. (We'll have more on this later.)

"I can't persevere." Yes, you can. Get some calluses on your knees. Get a spiritual director or someone you can talk to. Report your progress regularly to that person. You might want to get a support group of other Christians who are determined to persevere in prayer. Realize that prayer usually takes hard work, and stick with it. Use your will power. Rely on the Lord to make your efforts fruitful. Use the prayer-gifts you received through baptism in the Holy Spirit. Recall the Lord's admonition to his apostles on the Mount of Olives.

> Simon, are you asleep? Could you not watch one hour? Watch and pray that you may not enter into temptation; the spirit is willing, but the flesh is weak (Mk. 14:37-38).

Though prayer may be personal and spontaneous, there remain certain definite elements in prayer. There are methods of prayer.

There are many misconceptions about prayer. Some believe prayer is just thinking nice thoughts about God. Others believe prayer basically involves warm feelings. These people are missing the point. Furthermore, prayer does not consist merely in a series of mental or emotional calisthenics. Prayer is not a kind of self-improvement program or a technique for building up your self-image.

Prayer is communication with the Lord. It involves the investment of your whole self. It is placing yourself personally in God's presence.

Prayer can be described as having five elements.

Praise: acknowledging and worshiping the Lord for who he is.

Repentance: examining yourself honestly, recognizing your sinfulness, renouncing sin and turning to the Lord.

Thanksgiving: responding in gratitude for the things God has done, especially calling to mind the things he has done for you personally.

Listening: waiting patiently for the Lord to speak. You don't have to do all the talking. Prayer is a dialogue, a conversation.

Petition: asking the Lord for the things you need and for the things needed by others.

Prayer is more than talking at God. Prayer is meant to be two-way communication. We need to be quiet at times and allow the Lord to teach us and direct us. We need quiet time to develop a sense of the presence of the Lord.

I didn't always realize this. About a year after getting involved in the charismatic renewal, I accepted pastoring from a mature Christian. He told me that at times in prayer I should be quiet and listen to the Lord. I tried this and, after a week or two, I was astounded to receive on a regular basis brief, encouraging words from the Lord. "My son, do not worry. You are in my hands. Know that I am the Lord of your life." I received those words one day. On another day, I received these words: "My son, do not be weary with cares. I will refresh you." These are typical of the words I often receive if I am quiet and listen for the Lord to speak.

Three or four times, I was scolded in a loving way by the Lord. Each time, it really made a deep impression on me and I vowed to make some changes in attitude or action. I was grateful that the Lord thought enough of me to correct me and I continued to be open to his word.

Here's another story about prayer being two-way communication. A friend of mine asked his son how the lad's prayer life was going. The son confessed that he had stopped praying because God started talking to him about six months previously, and that frightened him. Of course, we should welcome communication from the Lord.

It's a good idea to develop a method of prayer. You can use it every day or only on occasions. Sometimes you might need structure in your prayer time and sometimes God might lead you to more spontaneity.

Here is one method of prayer that has proven fruitful.

1. Remember that you are in the presence of God.

2. Decide to be reconciled with anyone who has offended you or whom you have offended. Jesus said that if you are on your way to the altar and realize that someone has anything against you, you should be reconciled.

3. Invite the Holy Spirit to fill your heart.

4. Praise God spontaneously. Use the gift of tongues.

5. Ask the Lord to guide you to a passage in Scripture. Read it and meditate on it.

6. Praise God in song.

7. Reflect on what the Lord has done for you in your life.

8. Thank him for all these blessings.

9. Be still and listen for the Lord to speak to you. Wait patiently and trust in him. Remember the story of Elijah in the cave.

> And there he came to a cave and lodged there. . . . and behold, the Lord passed by, and a great and strong wind rent the mountains, and broke in pieces the rocks before the Lord, but the Lord was not in the wind; and after the wind an earthquake, but the Lord was not in the earthquake; and after the earthquake a fire, but the Lord was not in the fire; and after the fire, a still small voice. And when Elijah heard it, he wrapped his face in his mantle and went out and stood at the entrance of the cave (1 Kings 19:9-13).

The voice of the Lord is still and small. Listen for it. You will recognize it when you hear it.

10. Ask the Lord for another Scripture passage. Read it. Meditate on it.

11. Once more give thanks to God.

12. Pray for the needs of others. Be confident.

> Ask, and it will be given you; seek, and you will find; knock, and it will be opened to you (Mt. 7:7).

13. Thank God that he has heard your prayer.

14. Raise up your own needs to the Lord. Close with the Lord's Prayer.

Sometimes we sense God's presence very strongly during our prayer. This is often true for persons recently baptized in the Holy

Spirit. On these occasions, our prayer is very easy because we are drawn naturally to the goodness of the Lord.

At other times, the Lord seems very distant. These are "dry" periods in our prayer life. When this happens, it is important that we persevere with zeal. Faithfulness to the Lord in prayer at such times will bear much fruit.

Fluctuations between times of dryness and times of sensing God's presence are normal as we make progress in our prayer. Perseverance in prayer is the key, not the degree to which we feel the Lord's presence.

In summary, it is essential that we pray every day. We may need a special method to pray. All in all, we need to be faithful to prayer.

In prayer, we encounter God in a special way. We come away from prayer newly filled with the Spirit of God. In some way, we are like Moses coming down from his encounter with God on the mountain.

> When Moses came down from Mount Sinai, with the
> two tables of the testimony in his hand as he came
> down from the mountain, Moses did not know that
> the skin of his face shone because he had been talking
> with God (Ex. 34:29).

Discussion Questions

1. Read Mark 14:37-38. How often do you find it difficult to get in your daily prayer? How do you struggle against the flesh so the willing spirit can pray?

2. Read Matthew 7:7. Do you pray for specific intentions? How often does God answer your prayers? Why does God seem not to answer at times when you knock?

3. How can prayer be a conversation? Does God ever talk to you? How? Why is it important to have spontaneous prayer as well as formal prayer?

4. Give personal examples from your own prayer about the five elements of prayer: praise, repentance, thanksgiving, listening, petition. Are all of them important? Why?

5. Describe some of the difficulties in prayer you are experiencing. How are you overcoming them? How are you overcoming discouragement?

6. Describe your particular method of personal prayer. What special gifts has God given you to help you pray? What encouragement can you give others about personal prayer?

CHAPTER TWO:
READING SCRIPTURE

Daily Scripture Readings

1. Read Proverbs 4:10-13, 20-22. Picture God as a loving Father who wants you to be eternally happy and who has written a book of guidance and encouragement especially for you. Learn to treasure the Bible.

2. Read Psalm 119:1-16. Enter into the joy of the psalmist, praising God for his laws. Rejoice in the admonitions of the Lord to be found in Scripture.

3. Read John 14:21-24. What connection is there between loving Jesus and keeping his commandments? Can we say we love Jesus if we don't try to obey him? How can we obey him unless we are familiar with his instructions to us contained in Scripture?

4. Read Joshua 1:5-9. Put yourself in the place of Joshua. The responsibility for leading the chosen people has fallen on you. Consider the strength you will get from relying on the laws which God gave to your predecessor, Moses. Through this law, God is guiding your steps also.

5. Read Matthew 4:1-11. Think about the power of the Scriptures. Note the way the devil uses Scripture to try and trap Jesus. Observe the way Jesus uses the true sense of Scripture to refute the devil.

6. Read Romans 15:4. Consider how the words of the Bible—both the Old Testament and the New Testament—are as valid

today as they were when they were originally written many centuries ago. God does not change. His eternal plan for his creatures does not change.

7. Read Colossians 3:12-17. Meditate on this portrait of the Christian life. Consider verse 16 and see how the word of Christ, Scripture, is at the center of the Christian life.

Through the Bible, we learn about God. We should read, study and meditate on the Scriptures. The written word of God should become an integral part of our personal lives.

This is probably a familiar story. We had a huge family Bible at home, sitting on a lower shelf of a table in the living room. It was big and impressive, but we almost never looked at it. In my whole life, I think I saw someone looking at it only three times—and twice it was to check on something in the family tree inside the cover.

In college, I took a number of theology courses and really enjoyed them. Back in the 1950s in the Catholic colleges I attended, however, there were slim pickings as far as Scripture courses were concerned and I came away from school with a very weak background in the Bible.

Through a career of teaching English in high schools and then working on newspapers, I retained an interest in religion in general. I subscribed to several religious periodicals and was pretty well-informed on the latest happenings in the field. Yet I rarely read the Bible or biblical books and periodicals. Frankly, I found reading the Bible to be boring.

Then I was baptized in the Holy Spirit and this changed instantaneously. The Bible was no longer boring; it was very exciting. It was as though widescreen color and stereophonic sound had been added. The people in the Bible were real; the events were real. I cared about them. I wanted to know more about them. The Bible was no longer a stranger; it was my friend.

If you came to my house and looked at some of my old family photo albums, you'd probably be bored. You wouldn't care about Grandpa Charlie and Uncle Floyd and Aunt Helen. They're not your family. My brothers and sisters and I get a kick from looking at our old family photos. They're important to us. They bring back memories.

That's sort of the way I now view the Bible. Before, the biblical stories were about people I didn't know and didn't care about.

Now the Bible is alive with accounts of my dear brothers and sisters in the Lord. Their experiences are very important to me. What happened more than 1900 years ago has a great deal of relevance to what is happening to me today.

In this chapter, we will consider a number of ways to become more knowledgeable about Scripture and to live lives based on the Bible. The key is to allow the Holy Spirit to soften your heart and open up the riches of Scripture to you.

What has reading the Bible to do with our eternal destiny? What does Scripture say about Scripture?

Why were we created? What is the purpose of our lives? The answers to fundamental questions like these are to be found in the Bible. Our goal in life is to know Jesus Christ, to love him and to become like him by serving others. To attain this goal, we need to pray and we need to study the Bible.

We need guidance; we need direction. God speaks to us in the quiet of our hearts in personal prayer. God also speaks to us in the Bible. The Scriptures are a public record, inspired by God, of his revelation to the world through Jesus Christ. Being immersed in Scripture in a variety of ways is—along with personal prayer—a very significant part of Christian life.

To come to know the Word of God, Jesus, we should look to the written word of God, the Scriptures, to learn what the Father has revealed about himself through Jesus Christ.

Here's what Scripture says about Scripture.

Scripture lights the way.

> Thy word is a lamp to my feet and a light to my path (Ps. 119:105).

> All Scripture is inspired by God and profitable for teaching, for reproof, for correction, and for training in righteousness, that the man of God may be complete, equipped for every good work (2 Tim. 3:16-17).

Scripture brings life.

> My son, be attentive to my words; incline your ear to my sayings. Let them not escape from your sight; keep them within your heart. For they are life to him who finds them, and healing to all his flesh (Pr. 4:20-22).

Scripture reveals Jesus.

> You search the Scriptures, because you think that in
> them you have eternal life; and it is they that bear
> witness to me (Jn. 5:39).

Scripture reveals the Father.

> If a man loves me, he will keep my word, and my
> Father will love him, and we will come to him and
> make our home with him. He who does not love me
> does not keep my words; and the word which you
> hear is not mine but the Father's who sent me (Jn.
> 14:23-24).

> I am the way, and the truth, and the life; no one
> comes to the Father, but by me. If you had known
> me, you would have known my Father also; hence-
> forth you know him and have seen him (Jn. 14:6-7).

**How do we approach the Bible? Do we just pick it up and
start reading? How do we make Scripture a part of our day-to-day
lives?**

Scripture can and should be a central part of our lives. We need
to become biblically based people. This means primarily that we
are to pick up the Bible often and read it. We are to become familiar
with the Scriptures. The word of God is to be our close friend.

What else can we do besides reading the Bible?

We can study Scripture. Holy Scripture was written by a variety
of persons, each of whom was inspired by God to write as he did.
Each wrote in the language of his culture. To find out what God is
saying to the world through Scripture, it is helpful to study the text
carefully, giving some attention to the language the author used
and the cultural context in which he wrote.

The purpose of our study should not be knowledge for the sake
of knowledge. Some Scripture scholars are atheists or agnostics.
Expertise in biblical minutiae in itself is no guarantee of holiness or
biblical wisdom. Yet scholarly understanding of the Bible can help
us appreciate more of the divine wisdom in Scripture. We can hear
God speaking to us more clearly.

You can get a Bible commentary or a Bible dictionary and study
on your own. You can go to a Bible seminar. You can take Bible
classes or join a Bible study group.

Prudence should be exercised in choosing your Bible commentary or class or study group. Some groups are not Christian in the traditional sense. The Way International, Jehovah's Witnesses and Mormons do not believe that Jesus is God, for example.

It is also true that Christians come from many different denominations, each with specific approaches to the Bible. Generally speaking, you should stick with your denomination or tradition in selecting a Bible commentary or Bible study group.

We can meditate on Scripture. The Bible should not only speak to our minds, but also to our hearts. We should ask ourselves: "What difference will this text make in my life? How can I conform to the pattern of God's plan for the Christian life insofar as it is revealed here in the word of God?"

> This book of the law shall not depart out of your
> mouth, but you shall meditate on it day and night,
> that you may be careful to do according to all that is
> written in it; for then you shall make your way
> prosperous, and then you shall have good success
> (Josh. 1:8).

The end result of our daily Bible reading should not be merely to say: "Oh, isn't that interesting!" Our wills should be affected by the word of God. As we meditate on Scripture, our emphasis should be on conforming our wills, under the guidance and power of the Holy Spirit, to obey what God has said to us personally through his word. We should begin our meditation on Scripture with a prayer and keep the prayerful spirit as we read.

> Teach me, O Lord, the way of thy statutes, and I will
> keep it to the end. Give me understanding, that I may
> keep thy law and observe it with my whole heart (Ps.
> 119:33-34).

> If any of you lacks wisdom, let him ask God, who
> gives to all men generously and without reproaching,
> and it will be given him (Jas. 1:5).

We can memorize Scripture texts. As we commit selected verses to memory, we can make them a part of our daily lives through frequent repetition and meditation on them.

> Blessed be thou, O Lord; teach me thy statutes. With
> my lips I declare all the ordinances of thy mouth (Ps.
> 119:12-13).

Memorized Scripture texts can be very helpful in fighting temptation. Jesus used texts to rebuff the temptations of the devil. (See Matthew 4:1-11.) The Psalms also talk of this.

> With my whole heart I seek thee; let me not wander from thy commandments. I have laid up thy word in my heart, that I might not sin against thee (Ps. 119:10-11).

As we do spiritual battle, we should make great use of the "sword of the Spirit, which is the word of God" (Eph. 6:17). Keeping Scripture verses in mind can encourage us in our walk with the Lord.

> For whatever was written in former days was written for our instruction, that by steadfastness and by the encouragement of the Scriptures we might have hope (Rom. 15:4).

Scripture verses woven naturally—not artificially—into our conversation can encourage Christian brothers and sisters and can be a witness to other persons. We can proclaim our faith in a more personalized way in our conversations than by using T-shirts and bumper stickers.

There are many methods for memorizing Scripture. Pick one that works for you. Perhaps your church or denominational bookstore would have suggestions.

We can make Scripture part of our day-to-day lives. Memorization is very important for this, as is faithfulness to daily Bible reading. Perhaps we could have a framed Scripture verse in calligraphy or needlepoint on our desk or in a prominent place at home.

Some people always carry a pocket New Testament with them. This can be handy for brief snatches of prayer and it can let the world know where we stand. We should be people of the book.

> Let the word of Christ dwell in you richly; teach and admonish one another in wisdom, and sing psalms and hymns and spiritual songs with thankfulness in your hearts to God (Col. 3:16).

How am I ever going to do all this? How much time should I set aside for Bible reading and meditation?

When becoming more familiar with the Scriptures, you should not try to do too much right away. You may become overwhelmed with the commitment and give up all Scripture reading and study. Or you may never even get started because you think the task is too enormous. Here are some practical suggestions.

Set aside 20 minutes a day to read three chapters of the Bible. This should get you through the entire Bible in a year. Pray before you start, but then read through the text. Do not meditate on the verses or study the text.

A simple plan to accomplish this is to alternate between an Old Testament book and a New Testament book. Finish one book before starting the next one. There are also specially printed Bibles that are arranged to get you through all the books in a year's time.

You should probably stick with arranged Bibles or daily reading guides that are prepared by your own denomination. Roman Catholic Bibles, for example, have more books than Protestant Bibles have.

Set aside five to 15 minutes daily to meditate on a short section of Scripture. This can be part of your regular daily personal prayer. It might also be a short period before bedtime to meditate on a passage in preparation for the next morning's prayer. It is important that you stick to this practice on a regular basis and that you let the Lord form you by his word on a regular basis.

Have one hour of Bible study once or twice a week. This can be in a Bible study group or by yourself with a commentary. The goal is for you to make steady, even if slow, progress toward understanding exactly what Scripture says. You will need to become familiar with some of the basic tools for studying Scripture (historical background, meanings of unfamiliar words, how to read poetic passages, etc.). You will need some access to helpful resources (commentaries, dictionaries, etc.) when you come across a difficult section in your daily reading. Often, knowing something about the history of the times, the way people lived, the Jewish culture, etc., will aid you in understanding parts of the Bible. Make use of these resources as you are able, but do not get into the habit of substituting them for Scripture itself. As you go through the Bible, keep note of the sections that mean the most to you and return to them later, so the Holy Spirit can impress them deeply on your heart.

Discussion Questions

1. Read Proverbs 4:20-22. How can we keep the word of God in our hearts? How can Scripture lead us to life? Why can the Bible lead us to true happiness?

2. Read Romans 15:4. What truths relevant for today can we learn from the Old Testament? How can the New Testament writings give us hope today?

3. Describe the ways the Bible has come more alive since you were prayed with for baptism in the Spirit. What are your favorite books of the Bible? What are your favorite passages?

4. What Bible commentaries have you found helpful? What system do you use in reading and studying the Bible?

5. How do you meditate on Scripture? Are you able to apply the texts to your daily life? How easy is this?

6. How are you making the Bible a part of your day-to-day life? Do the people you meet know you read the Bible? What do they think about this?

Chapter Three:
THE LORD'S GUIDANCE

Daily Scripture Readings

1. Read 2 Timothy 3:14-17. Consider that the person well-versed in Scripture always walks in the light of God's word. Praise God for the instruction contained in the sacred writings.

2. Read Romans 8:28-39. Ponder the mystery of Providence. We cannot understand all the divine plans, but we can put our complete trust in him.

3. Read Hebrews 13:7-9, 17. Respect your pastors and heed their admonitions. Thank the Lord for providing others who are concerned for your spiritual welfare.

4. Read James 3:13-18. Look for guidance to those persons whose lives exhibit virtue. Have confidence in your decisions if they are accompanied by a sense of the peace of the Lord.

5. Read Judges 6:36-40. Know that God can direct our paths by extraordinary means. Pray for wisdom about when to ask for an extraordinary sign.

6. Read Proverbs 11:14 and 12:15. Consider the importance of listening to sound advice. Pray for humility to accept advice.

7. Read John 10:2-5. How do we know the voice of the Good Shepherd? How does he speak to us?

What is the Lord's plan for us? How can we know if we are following the Lord's will? How does he speak to us?

Several years ago, I was at a small prayer meeting. I was asked by the leaders to be available after the meeting to pray with anyone who requested prayers. A man came up and asked for prayers for discernment about a new career. I spent some time praying with him. When I opened the Bible for guidance, I came upon no Scripture passage that seemed particularly anointed by the Holy Spirit in the situation.

He came back at the next prayer meeting with the same request. I found out that he went to several prayer meetings a week, always seeking discernment about a career. He told me that he had quit a good job some months previously because he opened to some Scripture passages that indicated to him that he should quit. Now he was importuning God for a better job.

The problem was that, in my judgment and in the judgment of other mature Christians, he was not listening to God, he was telling God. Presumably, he wanted to quit his previous job and kept looking for passages until he got some that he could use to claim God wanted him to quit. He wanted to go into business for himself in a certain field. He kept searching for some Scripture passage to confirm that God was going to provide a living for him in this field.

This is an example of illuminism. Some people in the charismatic renewal sometimes rely too heavily on the spiritual gifts and on random Scripture passages for specific guidance and they ignore common sense and mature advice. A balanced approach must be taken. God does have a plan for us and we should make prudent efforts to discern it. Sometimes he wants to tell us plainly and directly. Sometimes he wants us to use the good sense he's already given us. Discernment and the counsel of others help us determine how God wants us to speak.

God sometimes does give us specific advice. We need to test it and then act on it. I was introduced into the charismatic renewal in 1974 at a prayer meeting in San Francisco run by John the Baptist Charismatic Renewal Community (JBCRC). At the time, it was the largest covenant community on the West Coast. In December, 1976, the community made a large commitment of money and personnel to open a charismatic renewal office to serve northern California. One man quit his job and was funded by the community to run the office. Retreats and teaching seminars were to be developed and scheduled. The group was pretty firmly committed in that location.

Just a few weeks later, during the first week of January, 1977, at a meeting of the leaders of JBCRC, strong words of prophecy came that the community should leave San Francisco. Community leaders prayed about this. Renewal leaders in several parts of the country were contacted and they prayed over the situation. The strong consensus was that this was, in fact, a word from the Lord. After further prayer and reflection, it was decided that the community should move to South Bend, Indiana, to join a larger community there, the People of Praise.

The last Sunday in February, at a special community gathering, all this was reported to the JBCRC membership. There was overwhelming support from the community. Several people came forward and said that the Lord seemed to be telling them the same thing recently.

Each person was to pray over the matter and make a decision about moving. My wife Dorothy didn't need much time. Even though she loved San Francisco very much, she was ready to start packing almost immediately. She asked me some questions about which furniture we should take. At the time, I was religion writer for the *Oakland Tribune,* and neither San Francisco paper had a religion writer. I felt a real commitment to serve the church in the Bay Area. I was reluctant to leave. I asked Dorothy to stop talking about which furniture we were going to take until I made up my mind that we were going to go.

I talked over the matter with one of the leaders of JBCRC and he suggested that I not let the matter drag on. I should pray for a couple of weeks at most and then make a decision.

The next day, Monday, during my prayer time, I asked the Lord for direction and heard nothing. During Tuesday prayer, I seemed to hear the faint voice of the Lord saying: "Go to South Bend." I didn't tell Dorothy about this. I tried to get in touch with one of the community leaders to discuss it, but was unable to contact him. Wednesday morning, I again asked the Lord what his will was for me. "I told you. Go to South Bend." The words almost seemed to be shouted in my ear. This shook me up, but I still was reluctant to make a firm commitment and tell my wife until I had talked it over with a leader of the community. Again, I was unable to get together with him.

Thursday morning, still not having made a firm decision, I again asked the Lord what his will was. I almost flinched, wondering if the answer would be very firm again. This time I heard a response, as it were, in a normal tone of voice: "Go to South Bend." "Yes, Lord," I said, "I'll go." That night I told my wife and later told the community leaders.

Dorothy also had a special word from the Lord about the move. I had asked her not to bring the subject up for a while, so we did not talk about it. Wednesday afternoon (the second day that the Lord had been speaking to me) she heard the Lord say to her: "Tell Ralph that what he is looking for here, he will find there." (In the circumstances, this meant that by giving up my job at the *Oakland Tribune*, I would find fulfilling and meaningful work in South Bend. This did happen.) Dorothy told the Lord: "You tell him. I'm not going to tell him." She shared this with me about a week later, after I had made my decision.

In the next few months, more than 90 members of JBCRC quit their jobs, sold their homes and moved to South Bend. That year, also, a number of other sizeable charismatic communities were prompted by the Lord to pack up and move to larger communities.

God gives us general guidance through his teaching in Scripture. We can also reflect on our lives and discern patterns of God's influence.

Scripture tells us that God is eager to give us guidance.

I will not leave you desolate; I will come to you (Jn. 14:18).

In all your ways acknowledge him and he will make straight your paths (Pr. 3:6).

We know that in everything God works for good with those who love him, who are called according to his purpose (Rom. 8:28).

There are three basic ways in which God gives us guidance in our lives:

1. Through him *teaching us*;

2. Through *our reflection* on our commitments and the general direction of our lives;

3. Through the *specific guidance* of the Holy Spirit here and now.

We are not talking about the sources of truth for our lives, but about how God can communicate his will for us about decisions that have to be made here and now. We are talking about how we

can discern God's will regarding specific courses of action. In doing
so, we will not be talking about all the ways God can guide us. We
will not be talking, for example, about obedience in religious orders
or about making a decision always to choose humility.

God is our teacher. Primary among the ways he teaches is
Scripture.

> All Scripture is inspired by God and profitable for
> teaching, for reproof, for correction, and for training
> in righteousness, that the man of God may be com-
> plete, equipped for every good work (2 Tim. 3:16-17).

> Thy testimonies are my delight, they are my counsel-
> ors (Ps. 119:24).

We also learn from our parents and other persons whom
Providence has placed in authority over us. These include pastors,
teachers and other Christian leaders.

> My son, keep your father's commandment, and
> forsake not your mother's teaching. Bind them upon
> your heart always; tie them about your neck. When
> you walk, they will lead you; when you lie down,
> they will watch over you; and when you awake, they
> will talk with you (Pr. 6:20-22).

> Obey your leaders and submit to them; for they are
> keeping watch over your souls, as men who will have
> to give account. Let them do this joyfully, and not
> sadly, for that would be of no advantage to you (Heb.
> 13:17).

**We can also learn from reading the lives of holy men and
women who have preceded us in the Christian walk. Their example can be a significant source of instruction for us.**

The Lord has also given his body the gift of teaching and other
gifts to guide us. The mature discernment of Christian leaders can
point out God's will for us.

> And his gifts were that some should be apostles, some
> prophets, some evangelists, some pastors and teach-
> ers, to equip the saints for the work of ministry, for
> building up the body of Christ, until we all attain to
> the unity of the faith and of the knowledge of the Son
> of God, to mature manhood, to the measure of the
> stature of the fulness of Christ; so that we may no

longer be children, tossed to and fro and carried
about with every wind of doctrine, by the cunning of
men, by their craftiness in deceitful wiles (Eph. 4:11-
14).

As we look to the future and seek what is God's will for our
lives, it can be helpful to look back and see how God has acted in our
lives in the past. What special blessings has he given us? How has
he supported us in time of tragedy or difficulty? How has he
guided us in decisions about marriage and career? When we reflect
back on the gifts that God has given us to serve him with and on the
special character he is trying to form in us, we can get deeper
insights into how the Lord would like us to serve him in the future.
We may not be called to be a bishop as Timothy was, but we have
been given specific Christian duties and responsibilities that we
need to be faithful to.

Do not neglect the gift you have, which was given
you by prophetic utterance when the council of elders
laid their hands upon you. Practice these duties,
devote yourself to them, so that all may see your
progress (1 Tim. 4:14-15).

Through it all, we should not get superspiritual about our
decisions. We also need to be practical. We need to be prudent. We
need to honor commitments already made. If we have a job, we
need to give our employer the hours of work we agreed to. If we are
married, we cannot decide on the spur of the moment to quit our
jobs or leave our homemaking responsibilities and take off for the
foreign missions. (Of course, the Lord may be calling some individuals to work exclusively in his vineyard.) It is usually not the
Lord's will for parents to leave children at home alone while they
go to three or four prayer meetings a week. We must prayerfully
consider our significant commitments as well as our serious responsibilities when we try to discern how to follow the Lord in the
future.

**At times, the Lord may prompt us directly regarding an
action. This is sometimes called a "leading of the Spirit." It may
take the form of a spiritual sense about the appropriateness of a
particular action or it may be a special sign or a prophetic word.**

In Acts 9:10-19, Ananias is instructed in a dream to go and lay
hands on Saul so that he could regain his sight. He obeyed these

instructions and was instrumental in Saul's being baptized and becoming the great apostle of the Gentiles, Paul.

Ordinarily, promptings of the Spirit are more subtle. They often take the form of a spiritual sense rather than any particular vision or prophetic word. The prompting could take the form of a gentle urging to go up to a stranger on the street and talk about the Lord. Or it could be a prompting to pray for a specific person or to call that person up and talk.

In general, we need to remain close to the Lord to feel these promptings. When they come, we should be willing to take some risks for the Lord. Of course, we should not do anything against Scripture or legitimate church teaching, but we should be bold, too. We always need discernment. The prompting could be coming from our own desires or from a scrupulous conscience or even from evil spirits. We need to test the prompting to see if it is from the Holy Spirit. There is a certain peacefulness that accompanies the genuine promptings of the Lord.

> But the wisdom from above is first pure, then peace-
> able, gentle, open to reason, full of mercy and good
> fruits, without uncertainty or insincerity. And the
> harvest of righteousness is sown in peace by those
> who make peace (Jas. 3:17-18).

The seriousness of the action we feel prompted to take is also a consideration. If it is simply the urge to talk to a stranger or to call up a friend, why not do it? There is little danger of bad consequences. More discernment is needed if the prompting involves a change in serious commitments.

At times, the Lord can guide us through signs. We may pray for a passage in Scripture and then open the Bible at random and see if the passage we look at seems to have something to say about our pending decision. Or we may be moved to "lay a fleece" before the Lord. In Judges 6:36-40, Gideon asked for a miracle to confirm that it was God's will that he lead the people into battle. He laid a fleece on the ground. The first morning the fleece was wet and the ground dry and the second morning the ground was wet and the fleece dry. This convinced Gideon that the Lord really wanted him to go into battle.

Sometimes it may be proper to "lay a fleece" before the Lord. When deciding whether to witness to a particular person, you might ask the Lord to prompt the person to call you. Or when deciding whether to accept a job at a particular office, you might say that you want a sign that the interviewer is a Christian.

"Laying a fleece" should not be the normal way of reaching a decision. This is not the ordinary way God reveals his will to us. Usually, there should be some sort of spiritual sense that now is the time to "lay a fleece." Signs can become a substitute for faith.

> The Pharisees came and began to argue with him, seeking from him a sign from heaven, to test him. And he sighed deeply in his spirit, and said, "Why does this generation seek a sign? Truly, I say to you, no sign shall be given to this generation" (Mk. 8:11-12).

Signs can become a substitute for really listening to the Lord and for using the natural means he has given us for discerning the right path. Our own desires can cloud our vision when we interpret the signs and we must remember that the enemy of our souls can control circumstances in various ways. The unusual circumstance seeming to be a sign may in reality not be due to God's intervention. Prudence and discernment are needed.

The Lord can offer us specific directions through the counsel of others, especially other members of the body of Christ.

Christians are joined together in the body of Christ. We have different gifts and different roles to play. We have different talents and different levels of maturity. Some are called to be leaders. Some are specialists in various fields. The Lord can offer us specific direction for our lives through the counsel of other persons, especially other members of the body of Christ. Scripture tells us that the wise man has many counselors.

> Without counsel, plans go wrong, but with many advisers they succeed (Pr. 15:22).

Christians should, whenever possible, seek advice on all major decisions. In seeking advice, we should look to persons with a mature faith and with some competency in the areas we are dealing with. Those experienced in a personal walk with Jesus will be able to help us be open to the light of Christ in our own lives in general and in some specific decisions in particular.

We may need to overcome any of several negative attitudes about receiving the Lord's guidance through others. Looking to others for help is seen as a sign of weakness in much of today's society. Rejection of authority, even authority which is based on greater competence, is often thought to be a sign of maturity and autonomy. We should act in the way we are shown in Scripture.

> The way of a fool is right in his own eyes, but a wise man listens to advice (Pr. 12:15).

> Where there is no guidance, a people falls; but in an abundance of counselors there is safety (Pr. 11:14).

There are dangers, of course, in looking to others for advice. You might get bad advice. You might become unduly dependent on the advice of others and become unable to make your own personal decisions and to accept responsibility for them. You may fall into the trap of shopping around for just the advice you want to hear and then go ahead and do what you wanted to do in the first place.

These dangers can be avoided. If we approach our decisions— and our asking for advice about the decisions—with a sense of responsibility for our own actions and a sincere and humble desire to know how we can best follow the Lord, we can avoid these difficulties.

Our trust must be in God, not in any method. We need to learn to recognize the Lord's voice.

No method is foolproof; all require discernment. If any method works, it is only because God chooses to enable us to discern his will that way. We are completely dependent on the Lord for guidance. God cannot be manipulated; we must trust him.

We should desire to know and to do God's will in every area. If we put his will first, valuing it more highly than our own, we will be better able to recognize it when we see it. We must decide to obey the Lord's will even before we know what it is. If we have a "wait and see" attitude, our vision will be clouded by our own desires.

On a daily basis, we need to reaffirm our commitment to follow the Lord unconditionally. If our desire for the Lord's will is not habitual, we will be unable to get our hearts right each time we need to discern his will.

We need to learn to recognize the Lord's voice, whether he is speaking to us immediately or through teaching, through circumstances or through other persons. We should reflect regularly on our experience of following the Lord. We should ask ourselves: how can I learn to be a better servant of Christ through what I have experienced? Through the study of Scripture and regular prayer, we can learn to recognize the Lord's voice.

> He who enters by the door is the shepherd of the sheep. To him the gatekeeper opens; the sheep hear his voice, and he calls his own sheep by name and leads them out. When he has brought out all his own, he goes before them, and the sheep follow him, for they know his voice. A stranger they will not follow, but they will flee from him, for they do not know the voice of strangers (Jn. 10:2-5).

I would like to conclude with another story about someone who followed leadings which came from the Lord. In 1975, I went to the international charismatic renewal conference in Rome. Some 10,000 persons came to that very significant gathering.

We had to make reservations early and pay for all expenses ahead of time. The chartered plane was totally sold out weeks before the departure date. My wife and I left fairly early in the morning for the Oakland airport. There I saw a number of other members of John the Baptist Charismatic Renewal Community and we had some excited conversations. We also met other people who were going on the flight and they were excited, too.

I noticed one man sitting quietly in the midst of all this excitement and anticipation. He had a quiet dignity about him, but he somehow seemed out of place. One of the ladies from our community went over and talked with him. She was excited when she came back to our group.

The man was from a prayer group in Los Angeles. He had not planned to go to Rome because he could not afford the trip. Several prophetic words and some prayerful discernment by the prayer group, however, indicated that it was God's will that he go to Rome.

Acting on these leadings and on his own sense for what God wanted, he took a step in faith. He flew up to Oakland, the West Coast point of departure for the conference, even though he had no ticket for Rome. By coincidence, a man from our community at the last minute decided that he was not going. So the man from Los Angeles took his place. He followed the indications of the Lord's will and things worked out for him. I understand from people on his bus that he was deeply moved by the conference and eager to share his enthusiasm with the members of his prayer group.

Discussion Questions

1. What is illuminism? When you make a decision, what part do reason and logic play? What part should advice from other Christians play in your decision-making? Read and discuss Proverbs 11:14 and 12:15.

2. Read 2 Timothy 3:16-17 and Psalm 119:24. How does the Bible guide us? Will the Christian who loves the Bible have an easier time discerning God's will than the Christian who rarely reads the Bible? Why? Can Scripture quotes be taken out of context?

3. Read Ephesians 4:11-16. Why should we trust the judgment of mature and tested Christian leaders? Is submission to legitimate pastoral authority wise?

4. Briefly look back over your life. Do you have an overall sense of God's guidance? Do you recall any special leadings of the Spirit that guided you at key times?

5. What do we mean by "laying a fleece"? Can this ever be helpful? What steps should be taken to forestall its abuse?

6. Discuss any decisions you arrived at through spiritual discernment. Did a particular Bible passage seem very significant? Were there words in prophecy or a gift of knowledge? Was there just a special spiritual sense? How did you test this discernment?

Section 2

Chapter Four:
THE WORLD

Daily Scripture Readings

1. Read Genesis 1:26-31 (or read all of Genesis chapter one). This is the story of the creation of the world. Note that in verse 31 and elsewhere in the chapter creation is seen as good. Give thanks to God the Father for the wonders of creation.

2. Read John 3:16-18. God shows his love for the world not only through the wonders of creation, but also by the infinite love he shows in sending his Son to save the world. Give thanks to God for creating the world and for saving the world.

3. Read 1 John 2:15-17. The world, for all its beauty, can be a source of temptation. It can lead us away from the Creator. Consider the dangers of the allurements of the world.

4. Read Romans 12:2. How should we look at the world? How do we know what is good? Where do we find the will of God manifested so we can judge the world by this criterion?

5. Read John 12:31-33. The "ruler of this world" is the devil. How can we consider the devil to be the ruler of the world? Why is the cross a powerful means of overcoming the temptations of the world?

6. Read John 15:18-26. What cost is there if we follow the Lord and not the world? Will we be criticized for turning our backs on the attractions of the world? How can we keep our resolve in the face of criticism?

7. Read Acts 2:44-47. How is Christian community a defense against the allurements of the world? What virtues did the members of the Acts community practice?

The Christian faces temptations from the world, the flesh and the devil. The world the Christian lives in is not usually a Christian world. The worldly environment offers many distractions to the Christian's walk with the Lord.

Traditionally, spiritual writers have grouped obstacles to the Christian path of virtue in three general categories: the world, the flesh and the devil. Temptations come from the material environment the individual lives in (the world), from the individual's own weak human nature (the flesh), and from spiritual enemies (the devil and his minions).

You gave your life to the Lord. You were baptized in the Holy Spirit. You are spending time in daily prayer and in reading the Scriptures faithfully. You might think that you will have easy sailing into the heavenly kingdom. Such is not the case, however. You are tempted, and you sin.

Christian traditions have different ideas about sin. Some Christians see sin everywhere. Even the committed Christian falls many times daily, they believe. Some liberal Christians, on the other hand, seem almost to doubt the existence of sin. Then there are Christians from some evangelical and Pentecostal backgrounds who maintain that, once converted, the individual cannot sin.

The position taken here is that, even after our conversion and even after being baptized in the Holy Spirit, we will be on a spiritual journey, a process of growth and development. In fear and trembling because of our weakness but confident in the love and mercy of God, we will *grow* in righteousness and holiness. In this process, we will have to deal with the problem of sin in our lives. That's not gone now that we have accepted Christ. In fact, our experience will show us that we do continue to sin.

Though in the next three chapters we will be talking about the world, the flesh and the devil, we don't want you to get discouraged. Jesus has won the victory. He has conquered sin and death. His grace is available for you. He is always ready to forgive your sins. We will talk about repentance and forgiveness in Chapter Seven.

We are often not aware of our environment. We take things for granted. The story of the frog and boiling water will illustrate this. (I've never tried this experiment, but the moral of the story is applicable.) If you drop a frog in a pot of boiling water, the frog will hop out immediately, not too much the worse for wear. If, on the other hand, you put the frog in a pot of cold water and gradually heat it to boiling, the frog will die. The change in the frog's environment is too gradual to be noticed.

A similar thing may be happening in our worldly environment. Unrighteousness and sin may have become so common that we don't even realize their existence and danger. I lived in San Francisco for many years and loved the city. I enjoyed the good aspects of life there so much that I came to overlook the bad aspects. When I took some friends from out of town to a nice restaurant on Broadway, however, I suddenly saw things from their viewpoint. The restaurant was in the middle of a row of striptease joints. We had to pass several of them on the way from the parking garage to the restaurant and I was embarrassed as the guys at the door tried to talk us into going inside.

Greed is very much a part of our national environment. We are urged to spend, spend, spend, not save, save, save. We are encouraged to borrow on our credit cards. Every few weeks I get another unsolicited advertisement for a national credit card and another opportunity to go into debt. Interest we earn through saving is taxed. The government is encouraging us to spend, not save.

In the United States, our standard of living is extremely high. Spending is a national pastime. In the world, hundreds of millions of people are on the verge of starvation. They live in hovels and have barely enough food to keep them alive. In the U.S., we spend $3.5 billion a year on cut flowers and $8 billion on pets.

Christians in the U.S. are very susceptible to this environment of greed and consumerism. A recent study by the Empty Tomb research organization, for example, showed that, in constant dollars, the average American had $2,511 more in disposable income in 1985 than in 1968, but the average member of 31 Christian denominations increased giving by only $49, just two percent of the additional income. Our greed grew faster than our income.

When Scripture speaks of "the world," it uses the word in several senses.

The story of creation in Genesis is an exuberant tale of God's love and care. It is the nature of love to be giving, to be creative. God's love impelled him, as it were, to create the universe and then to create humans to enjoy this marvelous creation. The world is good, as God created it. It should lead us back to God, not away from him.

> And God saw everything that he had made, and
> behold, it was very good (Gen. 1:31).

> For God so loved the world that he gave his only Son,
> that whoever believes in him should not perish but
> have eternal life. For God sent the Son into the world,
> not to condemn the world, but that the world might
> be saved through him (Jn. 3:16-17).

Some Christian writers believe that the world will not be destroyed at the end of time, but will be renewed and restored for the enjoyment of the saints who have risen from the dead. Whether it will happen that way or not, we should love and respect creation. We should enjoy the marvels of nature and take care of our environment. We should take time to appreciate the sunset as well as poems about the sunset. God made everything out of nothing and Jesus redeemed all creation. Christians should applaud and enjoy the good things God has created and the good things humans have made through the talents given them by the Creator.

That is the good news. Now comes the bad news. Scripture also talks about the world in a negative sense, as the environment we live in which espouses values, ideas and behavior which are opposed to the Christian life. We are influenced by the people and organizations we interact with. These influences are real whether we are conscious of them or not. We can be influenced for good or for bad by the world without being aware of it. Scripture talks bluntly about the negative influence of the world.

> Do not love the world or the things in the world. If
> anyone loves the world, love for the Father is not in
> him. For all that is in the world, the lust of the flesh
> and the lust of the eyes and the pride of life, is not of
> the Father but is of the world. And the world passes
> away, and the lust of it; but he who does the will of
> God abides forever (1 Jn. 2:15-17).

In this passage, the world is considered primarily in terms of the effects of sin it still bears. The world involves a complex set of relationships, ideas and values woven together in enmity with God. It is a major source of temptation and a bad influence on Christians and non-Christians alike. John judges the world severely in other passages also.

> We know that we are of God, and the whole world is in the power of the evil one (1 Jn. 5:19).

> Now is the judgment of this world, now shall the ruler of this world be cast out (Jn. 12:31).

It is this second meaning of "the world" that we will discuss for the rest of this chapter. We will talk about the ungodly environments and associations which take us away from the Lord and the life he calls us to. We will discuss ways to overcome the influence of the world.

Christians are not to be "conformed to this world, but transformed."

We need to recognize and resist those worldly influences which are contrary to the spirit of the gospel. We need to be strong and practice virtue.

> Do not be conformed to this world, but be transformed by the renewal of your mind, that you may prove what is the will of God, what is good and acceptable and perfect (Rom. 12:2).

What does the world tell us about *relationships?* It tells us to look out for number one. It tells us to be selfish. Giving honor is out; disrespect for authority is in. Commitments give way to current desires. Pride and unbridled ambition are extolled as motivating forces. For the Christian, on the other hand, importance is placed on self-sacrifice, on laying down one's life for one's neighbor. The Christian humbly recognizes legitimate authority and upholds the integrity of commitments.

In the realm of *ideas*, the world considers truth to be relative. (You believe in God. That's fine. I don't.) New Age philosophers extol a pantheistic vision of oneness and assail attempts at making distinctions between the true and the false. Everything is relative. On the other hand, the Christian knows that there is one ultimate truth. God and God's laws are real and at the end of time everyone will be judged according to these laws.

What *values* does the world promote? Advertising rarely talks about the intrinsic merits of a product. Ads appeal to self-indulgence, personal prestige, greed and the desire for power. In movies targeted at teenagers, who is the hero or heroine? Usually some rebellious twit with no respect for learning or honor or tradition. Who is the villain? Usually the nincompoop principal or teacher or parent. When is the last time you saw a clergyman or religious leader treated with respect in a movie or television program? It doesn't happen very often.

This country used to extol Judeo-Christian values. It seemed normal that a husband and wife would remain married and would raise a family. There was respect for authority. Honesty was important. A promise meant something. That is rarely the case now.

Organizations are often very worldly. The almighty dollar is in command. The sale must be made at all costs even if the product is defective or inappropriate for the customer. Christians often lament that they can't compete unless they also use dishonest sales techniques. How many organizations make family life a priority? To climb up the corporate ladder, how many Christians are forced to work 60- and 70-hour weeks and to move to a new locality every few years? Is the language at the workplace appropriate? Are women treated with dignity at work or are they subjected to sexual harassment? Many organizations are run by people who are at least nominal Christians, but what are they doing to see that their organizations operate with Christian values?

It's tough to be a practicing Christian in today's society. You don't get much encouragement from the world around you. If you feel out of place, however, you may just be doing things right.

> If the world hates you, know that it has hated me
> before it hated you. If you were of the world, the
> world would love its own; but because you are not of
> the world, but I chose you out of the world, therefore
> the world hates you. Remember the word that I said
> to you, "A servant is not greater than his master." If
> they persecuted me, they will persecute you; if they
> kept my word, they will keep yours also. But all this
> they will do on my account, because they do not
> know him who sent me (Jn. 15:18-21).

Those in the world recognize that you are from another environment. There is a real difference between the worldly and Christian environments. Those in the world intend to persecute those who follow the Lord. If you live as a Christian in the world, you can expect to be laughed at and scorned.

As you grow closer to Christ, you will discover more and more that many of your ways of relating, many of your ideas and many of your values have been formed by worldly environments and are contrary to Christian life. It is important that, as a Christian, you become aware of the influence that each of your environments has upon you—both the worldly environment and the Christian environment.

What can be done? How can Christians live in the world but not be overwhelmed by negative influences?

What steps should a follower of Jesus take to combat the harmful influences of the world?

Evaluate your environments accurately, one by one. How do they stack up in relation to Christian ideals? Consider your living situation, your job, your school, your social life. Some of these may be good, some indifferent, some slightly bad and some evil. Put on the mind of Jesus and honestly evaluate your environments. If he walked with you during the day, how would he react to the various situations you find yourself in?

Leave those environments that seriously hamper your walk with the Lord. If your living situation is sinful, change it. If your friends are into serious sin—fornication, drugs, pornography, theft— and if you are not strong enough to get them to change their ways, leave them. If your boss insists that you sell defective merchandise, get another job. If the language at work is extremely bad or the sexual harassment unbearable, go someplace else. If Christians are held up to scorn at your school so much so that you are afraid you will lose your faith, go to another school.

Cope as best you can with worldly environments that are not ideal, but that are not immediate occasions of sin, either. Be a force for good wherever you are. Tough as the going may be, Christians need to let their lights shine in the classroom, in the marketplace, in the home and in the street. See what you can do to influence or change the environment for the good. Employers, for example, are usually sensitive about charges of sexual harassment. Make friends in these various environments with other Christians and with people who affirm an honest and virtuous life.

Grow in virtue and spiritual strength. Be faithful to daily prayer and the regular reading of Scripture. Pray for the improvement of the environments you find yourself in and for wisdom about how to handle them. Look for books about living as a Christian in your state in life.

Get the support of a Christian environment. Get involved in your church or Christian fellowship. Find a Bible study group or a prayer meeting or a Christian social-action group that appeals to you. You may be attracted to a Christian covenant community. You need to spend some time regularly in a Christian environment to help you handle all the times you spend in a worldly environment. We are not meant to walk through this life alone. The love and joy and encouragement and support coming from Christian brothers and sisters are essential. That's the way God wants it to be.

> And all who believed were together and had all
> things in common; and they sold their possessions
> and goods and distributed them to all, as any had
> need. And day by day, attending the temple together
> and breaking bread in their homes, they partook of
> food with glad and generous hearts, praising God and
> having favor with all the people. And the Lord added
> to their number day by day those who were being
> saved (Acts 2:44-47).

Discussion Questions

1. Read Romans 12:2. How do you evaluate situations? What criteria do you use? Are you concerned about what God thinks about them? Or do you habitually rely on the opinions of secular experts? Explain.

2. Read John 15:18-21. How are Christians persecuted in foreign countries? How are Christians persecuted here at home? When and why would the world hate Christians?

3. What are some good things about the world we live in? Where can we find the good and the beautiful in creation?

4. How does the world look at Christians? How are Christian leaders portrayed on television and in the movies? What do *Time* and *Newsweek* think about Christians?

5. How can the world be an obstacle to a Christian's walk with the Lord? What sins arise from worldly temptations? Are the fundamental values of the world helpful or harmful to the Christian?

6. How do you feel when others learn you are a Christian? Are you embarrassed to stick up for your faith? What practical steps can you take to overcome this embarrassment?

CHAPTER FIVE:
THE FLESH

Daily Scripture Readings

1. Read Galatians 5:16-21. Have you ever experienced temptations to the "works of the flesh"? Pray to be able to walk always by the Spirit in the face of temptation.

2. Read Romans 7:14-25. Think about your intellect and will struggling with the desires of the flesh. Pray to God for perseverance to overcome these temptations.

3. Read Romans 8:5-9. Consider the plight of the worldly person. How can there be peace of mind without God? Thank God for the Spirit who dwells within you. Resolve to continue the struggle against the temptations of the flesh.

4. Read Ephesians 4:17-24. We can triumph over the flesh. We do not have to live as those who do not know Jesus. Ask Jesus to give you a new nature and a renewed mind. Ask Jesus to be Lord of your life.

5. Read Philippians 4:8-9. How can acts of virtue help us overcome temptations? How can daily prayer and regular Scripture reading keep us on the right path?

6. Read 1 Corinthians 9:24-27. Are we willing to train as hard as an athlete to obtain the spiritual prize? Are we willing to fast and practice self-discipline to grow in virtue?

7. Read Matthew 10:16-23. Are we strong enough to face persecution? Jesus did not promise that following him would always be easy. Are we prepared to endure to the end?

Not only do we have enemies from without tempting us to sin, but our own human nature is weak. Too often we fail to do what we really want to do.

In our spiritual walk, we are under attack from the world and from the devil. These are outside influences. We are also under attack from within. Our own weak, sinful human nature is a source of temptation. This weak human nature is sometimes called "the flesh" in Scripture, though this term has other meanings, too.

For those of us who are overweight, the term "the flesh" is so appropriate. I have gone on various diets many times over the years. I work and work at it and deny myself and suffer—and eventually I lose a few pounds. Then I go on a trip or on vacation or even out for a pizza with the guys and I gain it all back. In the first draft of this chapter, I wrote that I had dieted for several months and taken 14 pounds off. I said I didn't know how long it would last. Well, it lasted less than four months. As I write this I'm back up to my previous weight and resolving to try and take it off again.

The point about this tale is that my body seems to have a mind of its own. My intellect says I need to lose some weight, but my body keeps nibbling and tasting and eating. It wants what it wants. My flesh wages a relentless war against my good intentions.

My body wants its sleep. I enjoy prayer and I know I need to get in a half-hour of personal prayer every day. Still, I really have to struggle to get out of bed to start my prayer time. Once I get up and get going, it's not too bad, but getting up is usually very hard.

Anger is something else I have trouble with. I'm usually a pretty easy-going guy. I shrug off a lot of minor irritations. Yet when someone or something does get my goat, I can seethe about it for days even though I tell myself just to forget it. I want to growl or kick something. I am just furious. I have a difficult time shaking this anger. This is another example of my flesh rebelling against my intellect and my will.

I have trouble with temptations to lust. I have heard that a wise old monk once told a young monk that lustful desires will cease "several hours after one is buried in the grave." All around us— billboards, magazines, television—are temptations to lust and, if that were not enough, our own fertile imaginations can dream up plenty of temptations. It's a constant struggle to remain pure and virtuous.

These are just some of the ways the flesh is at war with the intellect and the spirit. Our motives can be the highest. We may truly desire to avoid laziness, gluttony, lust, greed, anger and other faults, but we fail again and again. We find that fleshly desires lead us in the opposite direction from the one we have consciously chosen.

What does Scripture say about the flesh? What does all this teach us about our fallen human nature?

We need to walk a middle road here. We should not despise our bodies. God created us, body and soul. The body and the bodily needs are good, but are disordered through sin. Unless we have a special call from God to be an ascetic, we should not flee to the desert and live on the barest necessities. On the other hand, we should not gratify our every fleshly desire and at the same time expect to grow rapidly in virtue. Prudence, moderation and firmness of purpose are necessary.

> But I say, walk by the Spirit, and do not gratify the desires of the flesh. For the desires of the flesh are against the Spirit, and the desires of the Spirit are against the flesh; for these are opposed to each other, to prevent you from doing what you would. . . . Now the works of the flesh are plain: fornication, impurity, licentiousness, idolatry, sorcery, enmity, strife, jealousy, anger, selfishness, dissension, party spirit, envy, drunkenness, carousing, and the like (Gal. 5:16-17, 19-21).

Paul does not beat around the bush. He is quite clear, quite detailed and quite specific. The flesh refers to an aspect of human nature in its fallen condition. He mentions sexual temptations and sins as well as many other weaknesses. The flesh is not simply a state of mind, a human point of view. The flesh is a powerful pull from the depths of one's fallen human nature.

Because of the sin of our first parents, there exists within us a lack of built-in self-control. We find within ourselves something like an unruly condition. In the human being there is an inclination to evil, an inclination to choose the lesser of two goods or to choose evil over good.

(Those with an interest in theological discussion may wish to delve into this subject further. A key point in the Protestant Reformation is at issue here. Some Protestants teach that, as a result of the fall, human nature is totally corrupt. Human nature can do no good; it is inherently sinful. Roman Catholics, on the other hand, teach that human nature remains basically good, though wounded and weakened by original sin. As a result, in our wounded human nature there is an inclination to sin. We will not pursue this theological discussion in this book. Suffice it to say that both Protestants and Catholics acknowledge our need in our fallen condition for the saving grace that comes through the death and resurrection of Christ. Both acknowledge the need for repentance and the importance of the virtuous life.)

We are pulled this way and that by our drives, emotions and passions. Our desires reach out to all kinds of things. Often our desires are drawn toward evil, despite what we know to be right and what we have decided to do. When we give in to these desires, we sin.

> We know that the law is spiritual; but I am carnal,
> sold under sin. I do not understand my own actions.
> For I do not do what I want, but I do the very thing I
> hate. Now if I do what I do not want, I agree that the
> law is good. So then it is no longer I that do it, but sin
> which dwells within me. For I know that nothing
> good dwells within me, that is, in my flesh. I can will
> what is right, but I cannot do it. For I do not do the
> good I want, but the evil I do not want is what I do.
> Now if I do what I do not want, it is no longer I that
> do it, but sin which dwells within me. So I find it to
> be a law that when I want to do right, evil lies close at
> hand. For I delight in the law of God, in my inmost
> self, but I see in my members another law at war with
> the law of my mind and making me captive to the law
> of sin which dwells in my members. Wretched man
> that I am! Who will deliver me from this body of
> death? Thanks be to God through Jesus Christ our
> Lord! So then, I of myself serve the law of God with
> my mind, but with my flesh I serve the law of sin
> (Rom. 7:14-25).

Paul is describing the condition of a dedicated Christian. He is describing a battle that is going on inside himself between the flesh and his will to do what is right. In this text, the flesh is the "law at

war with the law of my mind" and the "law of sin in my members."
It seems clear that Paul is not only talking about himself, but means
to say that all Christians undergo this struggle. "The flesh" refers
to the inclinations of our unruly passions and drives to do that
which is evil.

"The desires of the flesh are against the Spirit" (Gal. 5:17). The
flesh is antispiritual and pulls us away from the spiritual and from
the work of the Holy Spirit in us.

> For those who live according to the flesh set their
> minds on the things of the flesh, but those who live
> according to the Spirit set their minds on the things of
> the Spirit. To set the mind on the flesh is death, but to
> set the mind on the Spirit is life and peace. For the
> mind that is set on the flesh is hostile to God; it does
> not submit to God's law, indeed it cannot; and those
> who are in the flesh cannot please God. But you are
> not in the flesh, you are in the Spirit, if in fact the
> Spirit of God dwells in you. Anyone who does not
> have the Spirit of Christ does not belong to him (Rom.
> 8:5-9).

**How can we win the victory over our flesh? Why is it impor-
tant to proclaim Jesus as Savior and Lord of our lives?**

We need to yield to God's Spirit in order to become a new
creation. Although Christ won the victory for us on the cross, we
need to incorporate that victory as an ever-increasing part of our
lives. Making that victory our own is a process. It doesn't happen
overnight or in a short period of time.

Many people are eager to accept Jesus as Savior, but slow to
accept him as Lord. Anyone who is in trouble will accept a savior.
A drowning man will clutch eagerly at a lifeline. Someone in a
burning building will welcome the fireman. When people hear the
gospel proclaimed and are convicted of sin and realize they face
damnation, they are eager to renounce their sins and accept the love
and forgiveness of the crucified Jesus.

To accept Jesus as Lord is a much bigger step. Accepting his
lordship over our lives means accepting his revealed will as to how
we are to behave and live and think. We not only clutch the lifeline,
we pull ourselves out of the water and change our whole way of
living to follow in the footsteps of the Master.

> Put off your old nature which belongs to your former
> manner of life and is corrupt through deceitful lusts,
> and be renewed in the spirit of your minds, and put
> on the new nature, created after the likeness of God in
> true righteousness and holiness (Eph. 4:22-24).

If Jesus is Lord of our lives, he is Lord of our relationships. We must forgive and be reconciled to anyone who has hurt us. If Jesus is Lord of our families, the husbands and wives will love and honor one another. The parents will correct and encourage and love the children and the children will treat one another with respect; they will love one another and love their parents.

If Jesus is Lord of our money, we will be generous to the church and to the poor. We will not spend money foolishly. If Jesus is Lord of our entertainment, we will never offend him in this sphere of activity. We will use leisure times to bring family and friends closer together and closer to their Lord.

Accepting Jesus as Lord of our lives allows for no exceptions. Nothing is exempt. Nothing is deliberately left under the dominion of sin. We do everything as though we were conscious of Jesus standing beside us, watching us and encouraging us. We don't straddle the fence. We give our whole lives to our Lord and Savior, Jesus Christ.

Allowing Jesus to be Lord of every aspect of our lives is impossible except through the power of the Holy Spirit, so we need to allow the Holy Spirit to influence us. The practices encouraged in the first two chapters of this book are also helpful. The more we read and study Scripture, the more we will learn about God's will in general and God's will in particular for our situations. Prayer will help us clarify God's will for us and will help strengthen our wills to follow the path of virtue.

We should cooperate with the Holy Spirit in taking dominion over the desires of the flesh. When temptation comes, we need to: 1. catch it early; 2. reject it firmly; 3. accept God's plan.

1. *Catch it early.* We need to be constantly alert. We need to recognize as soon as we can that we are being tempted. We need to "take every thought captive to obey Christ" (2 Cor. 10:5). Daily, perhaps as part of our regular prayer, we should take stock of our lives and actions. We need to be aware of the traps we often fall into and the problems that we encounter regularly. We need to have an accurate picture of our personal strengths and weaknesses.

2. *We must firmly reject* whatever is wrong in our thoughts and

attitudes. Besides saying "No! No! No!" to the temptation, we can also take positive actions. We can distract ourselves. We can force ourselves to think of something else, perhaps something in marked contrast to the temptation. If we are getting angry, we can think of something funny or light-hearted. If we are tempted by lustful thoughts, we might think of sports or hobbies or something else entirely different from the temptation.

> Whatever is true, whatever is honorable, whatever is just, whatever is pure, whatever is lovely, whatever is gracious, if there is any excellence, if there is anything worthy of praise, think about these things (Phil. 4:8).

We need to pray for strength in general and for the grace needed to resist any particular temptation that may be plaguing us. Pray regularly for an increase in virtue.

Self-discipline is also very important in resisting difficult temptations. Regular fasting and almsgiving help train our wills. Mortification helps us keep our flesh under control. We should imitate the example Paul gives us.

> Do you not know that in a race all the runners compete, but only one receives the prize? So run that you may obtain it. Every athlete exercises self-control in all things. They do it to receive a perishable wreath, but we an imperishable. Well, I do not run aimlessly, I do not box as one beating the air; but I pummel my body and subdue it, lest after preaching to others I myself should be disqualified (1 Cor. 9:24-27).

There's a spiritual payoff to self-discipline. Not only will personal sacrifices strengthen the will, they will strengthen our virtue. We will have more spiritual power to resist difficult temptations.

We need to avoid those things and those situations that especially cause us temptations. For years, I knew I had to be cautious about seeing movies that were very sexy, but I felt I usually could see a movie that was very violent without too much ill effect. Lately, however, I am coming to realize that I must use some caution about violent movies, too. They can adversely affect my prayer life and the tranquillity I need in order to write on spiritual matters.

It is not prudent to flirt with danger. In Old Testament times, the Jews made rules of life that were even stricter than the letter of the law. By following these rules, the people would have less chance of offending against the law itself. They called this "putting a fence around the law." The Pharisees eventually went too far and gave the force of law to these protective rules. We should not go to excess, but it is good at times to "put up a fence" and avoid near occasions of sin. We need to protect ourselves.

3. *Accept God's plan* for your lives and seek to keep God's will for you always in your minds to guide you. Act on this knowledge. Our daily prayer and daily reading of Scripture will help keep God's plan always before us.

Finally, we should attack temptations of the flesh with courage and energy and with clarity and truth.

> Strengthen the weak hands, and make firm the feeble knees. Say to those who are of a fearful heart, "Be strong, fear not! Behold, your God will come. . . and save you" (Is. 35:3-4).

> He who endures to the end will be saved (Mt. 10:22).

We need courage. We need to be energetic and determined. If we are lazy and timid, we will be in danger of succumbing to temptation. If we are tempted in one area of our lives, we can act in the opposite way. If we are tempted to anger, we can force ourselves to be especially kind and patient. If we are tempted to gossip, we can resolve to go out of our way to say good things about people.

We need to be ruthlessly honest with ourselves. God knows the true situation; why should we try to kid ourselves? In your Scripture reading, note the very frank and straightforward way Jesus dealt with people. We should be just as frank with ourselves.

Discussion Questions

1. Read Galatians 5:16-21. Why are the desires of the Spirit opposed to the desires of the flesh? Can we be both selfish as well as generous? Are we allowed to be selfish sometimes? Are you tempted by the works of the flesh listed by Paul?

2. Read Romans 7:14-25. Is Paul being too harsh when he says: "I know that nothing good dwells within me, that is, in my flesh"? How is the law of God at war with the law of sin?

3. Read 1 Corinthians 9:24-27. Why is self-discipline important

in combatting the flesh? How does will-power work along with the grace of God to overcome temptation?

4. Why is it important to accept Jesus as Lord as well as Savior? What practical steps can we take to make Jesus Lord of our lives?

5. Why can it be wise to "put up a fence" around temptations and avoid even the near occasions of sin? If we flirt with danger, is it likely that we will fall into sin sooner or later?

6. Have you made special sacrifices during Lent or at other times? Has this practice helped you grow closer to God? Have you ever fasted? Does this have a spiritual effect?

Chapter Six:
THE DEVIL

Daily Scripture Readings

1. Read Revelation 12:7-12. Note the power of the devil and the greater power of Michael and his angels. Know that the power of God is much greater yet. See that the devil has power to cause many problems on earth, but that he has been conquered by the blood of the Lamb.

2. Read Isaiah 14:12-15. This passage is often taken as referring to the fall of Satan from heaven. Think of the reality of Satan and his power and call upon the Lord Jesus to save you and protect you.

3. Read Job 1:8 to 2:10. Even though God permitted Satan to afflict Job, Job did not sin. God also put limits on the actions of Satan.

4. Read Mark 5:1-20. Note the power of the demonic spirits and the much greater power of Jesus. Pray that you be kept from the power of the evil one.

5. Read Ephesians 6:10-18. Consider carefully the various ways we can combat the attacks of the enemy. Why should we be confident of victory over the devil?

6. Read 1 Peter 5:6-11. Is the devil really as dangerous as a roaring lion? What can we do to resist him? Why is humility a key virtue in our struggle with the devil?

7. Read Luke 10:17-20. As a believer, how can you exercise authority over evil spirits? What should you principally rejoice in?

How powerful is the devil? How much influence does he have in our lives? What temptations come from the devil? What are the signs of spiritual warfare?

An acquaintance of mine, an inmate, was assigned to work with the Protestant chaplain at a large state prison in the Midwest. He told me they were happy if 15 inmates showed up for the Sunday Protestant service. About 60 attended the Sunday Catholic Mass. There were about 600 Satanists in the prison, he said, and they regularly met several times a week.

An ABC-TV news documentary, *20/20*, broadcast May 16, 1985, included a segment on the spreading and dangerous phenomenon of Satan worship. The television program included testimony of former cult practitioners and interviews with police investigators, suggesting strongly that ritual murder may be a major element in such activities.

An article by Brian Peterson in the October, 1988, *Charisma & Christian Life* asserts:

> The number of ritualistic crimes appears to be increasing . . . , more Americans, particularly adolescents, are dabbling in occult-related activities . . . .

> An increasing number of law enforcement officers are taking the problem (of Satanism) seriously because more church vandalism, animal sacrifice and sexual assaults carry the signs of being occult-related. In addition, most criminal investigators have noticed an increase in Satanic-related homicides . . . .

Author and researcher Ted Schwartz has spent five years interviewing law enforcement officers, former Satanists and victims of satanic abuse. His conclusion: Satanism exists in some form in every community. One of his greatest concerns is Satanist workers in daycare centers.

An Associated Press story reported that five men were arrested and charged with 169 counts of child sexual molestation and abuse, and a prosecutor said authorities were investigating whether the suspects made a "snuff movie" in which children were killed on camera. One newspaper reported that it had learned that the sexual activities with the children centered around "Satanic worship."

There is also a rising contemporary fascination with witchcraft, magic, paganism and the occult. We need to have a clear understanding of the devil and all his works from a Christian perspective.

Some people don't believe in the devil. They think he's a myth. Others believe just the opposite. They see the devil personally behind everything bad that happens.

There are many different ideas about the devil. Here are some of them.

1. Some say the devil is a *myth*. God is also a myth. Neither God nor the devil really exists, but humans have made up stories about them over the years.

2. Others believe there are two contrasting creative forces in the universe, a principle of good and a *principle of evil*. There is a good god and a bad god, one as powerful as the other. Often more attention is paid to efforts at placating the evil god than at pleasing the good god.

3. Some Christians have only a *vague idea* about the devil. They often also have only a vague idea about God. Their faith tells them there is a God and a devil, but these concepts mean little to them in practical terms.

4. Some Christians see *the devil everywhere*. Some go so far as to believe that the devil is controlling everything and God has a hard time accomplishing anything. The devil rules this age and we are practically powerless to act. Prayers of deliverance may become the center of their spirituality.

5. Other Christians believe *the devil is completely powerless* to affect a Christian. Once a person has been baptized and has accepted Jesus as Lord and Savior, the devil is completely helpless. Once a person is covered by the blood of Jesus, the devil stays away. He afflicts unsaved people, not Christians.

6. Our viewpoint in this book is that *the devil is powerful, but no match for God*. Evil spirits are fallen angels, God's creatures, who are completely subject to the Creator. God's providence allows evil spirits to plague humans—including Christians—at times, but the evil spirits can be controlled and driven off by claiming the power of Jesus.

The devil and all other evil spirits are fallen angels and very powerful. Jesus' death on the cross, however, has given us victory over the enemy and his works.

In the previous two chapters, we looked at the negative influences of the world around us and at the tendency toward sin in our own flesh. Now we are considering the third source of sin and disorder in our lives—the work of the devil and his evil spirits.

The devil and all other evil spirits are fallen angels. All angels were created by God. Some of them sinned and were cast out of God's presence. The devil is Satan or Lucifer, the principal fallen angel, and evil spirits are other fallen angels.

> Now war arose in heaven, Michael and his angels
> fighting against the dragon; and the dragon and his
> angels fought, but they were defeated and there was
> no longer any place for them in heaven. And the
> great dragon was thrown down, that ancient serpent,
> who is called the Devil and Satan, the deceiver of the
> whole world—he was thrown down to the earth, and
> his angels were thrown down with him (Rev. 12:7-9).

> And the angels that did not keep their own position
> but left their proper dwelling have been kept by him
> in eternal chains in the nether gloom until the judg-
> ment of the great day (Jude 1:6).

Some Christian writers have seen some verses of Isaiah 14 as recounting the fall of Lucifer. The literal meaning of the passage is a prophecy about the king of Babylon. Using an accommodated sense of Scripture, the writers see the text as also referring to Satan. Some translations have "Lucifer" instead of "Day Star."

> How you are fallen from heaven, O Day Star, son of
> Dawn! How you are cut down to the ground, you
> who laid the nations low! You said in your heart, "I
> will ascend to heaven; above the stars of God I will set
> my throne on high; I will sit on the mount of assem-
> bly in the far north; I will ascend above the heights of
> the clouds, I will make myself like the Most High."
> But you are brought down to Sheol, to the depths of
> the pit (Is. 14:12-15).

The devil may be fallen but he's still an angel, and angels by nature are more powerful than humans. The second letter of Peter calls angels "greater in might and power" (2 Pt. 2:11) than humans. The devil, the most powerful of the fallen angels, is called the "ruler of this world" (Jn. 12:31) for he is more powerful than any creature on earth. We are no match for the enemy if we rely only on our natural powers or on other kinds of human wisdom.

Sometimes, as in the movie *The Exorcist*, the devil is depicted as being nearly as powerful as God. This is not the case. God is fully sovereign over all creation in general and over the devil and evil spirits in particular. Even as his darkest hour was approaching, Jesus said that "the ruler of this world . . . has no power over me" (Jn. 14:30).

The enemy only has power because God permits it. God restrains him as if he were on a leash.

> Then Satan answered the Lord, "Does Job fear God for nought? Hast thou not put a hedge about him and his house for all that he has, on every side? Thou hast blessed the work of his hands, and his possessions have increased in the land. But put forth thy hand now, and touch all that he has, and he will curse thee to thy face." And the Lord said to Satan, "Behold, all that he has is in your power; only upon himself do not put forth your hand." So Satan went forth from the presence of the Lord (Job 1:9-12).

Jesus' death on the cross gives us victory over the devil and his works. Thus, in any given temptation, he provides us with the grace to resist and overcome the temptation.

> God is faithful, and he will not let you be tempted beyond your strength, but with the temptation will also provide the way of escape, that you may be able to endure it (1 Cor. 10:13).

> Submit yourselves therefore to God. Resist the devil and he will flee from you (Jas. 4:7).

The Christian life involves spiritual warfare. The devil works for the downfall of individuals in an organized way. The devil also works to foster wars, immorality and false teaching.

The devil and his evil spirits are at war against God and against us. They have significant influence in the world.

> For we are not contending against flesh and blood, but against the principalities, against the powers, against the world rulers of this present darkness, against the spiritual hosts of wickedness in the heavenly places (Eph. 6:12).

Satan and his evil spirits oppose the work of God everywhere, wielding whatever weapons they can find and use effectively. They can even use things which are good in themselves. "Even Satan disguises himself as an angel of light" (2 Cor. 11:14). The devil can use such good things as human love, nature, sports, literature, art or music to draw people away from God and into sin.

Satan is relentless in his striving to thwart God's purposes. The enemy tries to keep us from salvation. If he cannot succeed in that area, he tries to keep those who are saved from rendering effective service to God.

The enemy works *in the lives of individuals*. He works for our downfall in an intelligent and organized way. Since they are creatures, the evil spirits are limited in their powers. They cannot, for example, directly read our minds, but they can observe character traits and personalities, hoping to pick up weaknesses. They can also manipulate our imaginations and emotions to some extent. The enemy can gain a foothold in our lives through sin, through fear or through such traumatic experiences as an accident or a fire. Evil spirits may gain entry through whatever hinders us from living in peace with God. They will also seek to find a way to influence us as they observe us struggling with the weakness of our flesh and the allurements of the world.

Using his influence over individuals and his keen grasp of circumstances, the devil works *in the world* to spread rebellion, disorder and every kind of evil. In this way, the "ruler of this world" affects the course of world events and the social order. He works to foster wars, crime, immorality of every kind and the spread of false ideologies. He works to foster bondage, all injustice and all the resulting poverty, hunger and violence. The enemy even works to erode the foundations of the church, fostering false doctrine and false moral teaching.

How does the devil operate? What are some signs that spiritual warfare may be occurring?

The devil will operate in whatever way he thinks he can thwart God's work. Sometimes he will operate openly through instilling fear or fostering lies. At other times, he will operate subtly in a hidden, disguised manner. Some of the obvious works of the enemy include the occult, bizarre phenomena and irrational impulses.

If we look around us, we can see that interest in the *occult* in general and the devil in particular is growing. Most larger cities have at least one occult or metaphysical bookstore. Items on sale include how-to books and paraphernalia for witchcraft rituals and satanic rites. Ordinary bookstores have suddenly introduced New Age sections, which include books on channeling, which is the consulting of demonic spirits. Open your newspaper to the movie ads. Go to certain sections of record stores. There are movies and albums glorifying Satan. Album covers and movie ads use such symbols as the broken cross or the upside-down cross. Anti-Christian rituals, such as the black mass, are extolled. Suicide and immorality are also extolled.

Ironically, Christians, who should be in the forefront of opposition to these developments, are not making much of a difference. A few years ago, I went to the library of a large Christian university to see what Christian writers were saying about the devil. I consulted four or five periodical indexes. I found almost a total silence about the devil in contemporary Christian publications. One popular missions magazine had a few articles on the devil and one professional missions publication had an article which, in effect, discounted the devil's influence. That was it.

Walter R. Martin, an anticult writer, uses the analogy of a door in talking about demonic spirits. The evil spirits are kept away from us by a door, as it were, and they do not have a doorknob on their side to open it. We do have a doorknob, however. Once we open the door, anything and everything can come through. You may only dabble in the occult by consulting a fortune-teller or using a Ouija board, but you have thereby opened the door to the whole occult world. If you have dabbled in the occult in any way and even if this happened years ago, you must be careful to renounce the practice completely. Chase out any lurking demonic influences through the power of the Holy Spirit and close, as it were, the door to the occult once again.

Bizarre phenomena may be the work of the devil. We are talking about things completely out of the ordinary. These could be abnormal sensory images like hallucinations or the strong experience of an immediate presence of personal evil. These may be due to demonic influences or they could be caused by complex psychological and physiological factors. Maybe there is a rational explanation to something that seems bizarre at the time. If there is demonic influence, the enemy may be producing the effects by himself or in conjunction with natural causes.

Irrational impulses may be explainable simply as psychological urges or they may be caused by the enemy. Sometimes these are irrational impulses to commit suicide or to hurt oneself or others. The impulse to speed up the car and drive off the road or to jump off a bridge or to cut oneself with a knife are typical examples. There are many possible psychological reasons for these impulses, but demonic activity can also be a factor.

The influence of the enemy may be subtle. The devil also works through temptations by the world and by the flesh.

Lying is central to the work of the devil, the "father of lies" (Jn. 8:44). All temptations are essentially lies. We are tempted to pursue an apparent good rather than a real good.

Poor self-esteem is basically a lie and it may be the root of many psychological and spiritual problems. Poor self-esteem may be due to demonic influence. Despair may result if we are made to forget God's love and forgiveness and to believe the lie of our worthlessness.

Many sins and bad habits are based on lies. A temptation to greed may be disguised as a perception of a just reward: "The Lord wants to bless you." We can justify selling defective merchandise because our family needs the income. We can justify selling a good product or service through dishonest sales presentations because the end seems to justify the means.

Lying can tear apart a Christian community. Rumors and slander and gossip can be deadly. To combat this, we need to stress right speech and we need to emphasize the truth. We may also need to pray against the attacks of the "father of lies."

Addictions often involve the influence of evil spirits. Though there are many other factors involved (like the world and the flesh), spiritual discernment has shown that evil spirits are sometimes at the root of addictions to alcohol and narcotics. Compulsive habits of eating, gambling and immorality are sometimes due to demonic influence.

I realize this may be hard to believe. People are going to say that there are perfectly natural explanations why people get drunk and commit fornication. This is true. It is also true that in praying for people, especially in the context of receiving baptism in the Spirit, demonic activity is often discerned as connected with the addiction. The devil ultimately may have been the one who trapped the individual in patterns of wrong behavior.

The enemy can cause both physical and mental *illnesses*. Deliverance from evil spirits was associated with some of the healings of Jesus.

> Now when the sun was setting, all those who had any
> that were sick with various diseases brought them to
> him; and he laid his hands on every one of them and
> healed them. And demons also came out of many,
> crying, "You are the Son of God!" But he rebuked
> them and would not allow them to speak because
> they knew he was the Christ (Lk. 4:40-41).

You will note that there is a distinction in Scripture between physical illness and affliction by evil spirits, as the passage above illustrates. Another example of this is in Mark 1:32: "That evening, at sundown, they brought to him all who were sick or possessed with demons." In the Gospels, Jesus never debates with an illness, but he sometimes talks with demons before casting them out.

> They came to the other side of the sea, to the country
> of the Gerasenes. And when he had come out of the
> boat, there met him out of the tombs a man with an
> unclean spirit, who lived among the tombs; and no
> one could bind him anymore, not even with a chain;
> for he had often been bound with fetters and chains,
> but the chains he wrenched apart, and the fetters he
> broke in pieces; and no one had the strength to
> subdue him. Night and day among the tombs and on
> the mountains he was always crying out, and bruising
> himself with stones. And when he saw Jesus from
> afar, he ran and worshipped him; and crying out with
> a loud voice, he said: "What have you to do with me,
> Jesus, Son of the Most High God? I adjure you by
> God, do not torment me." For he had said to him,
> "Come out of the man, you unclean spirit!" And
> Jesus asked him, "What is your name?" He replied,
> "My name is Legion, for we are many." And he
> begged him eagerly not to send them out of the
> country. Now a great herd of swine was feeding
> there on the hillside; and they begged him, "Send us
> to the swine, let us enter them." So he gave them
> leave. And the unclean spirits came out, and entered
> the swine; and the herd, numbering about two

> thousand, rushed down the steep bank into the sea,
> and were drowned in the sea (Mk. 5:1-13).

If the person has a physical or mental illness, pray for healing. If the person is afflicted by demons, pray for deliverance from the demonic attack. Discernment is needed to focus our prayer on the real problem.

Problems in the spiritual life such as scrupulosity or spiritual pride can be fostered by the enemy. Some *emotional problems* or confusion may, at times, be due to the work of the devil.

In these matters, we need always to think and act prudently. Not everything that is bad or seems bad is caused by the devil. Our own vices are the cause of many of our sinful actions. The world and the flesh tempt us and sometimes we fall. We need to discern accurately the underlying cause of the evil. Also very helpful is the discernment of other mature Christians who can objectively evaluate our situation, using prudence and the gift of discernment which comes from the Holy Spirit.

How can we overcome the work of the enemy? How can we fight the attacks of the evil one?

To gain victory over the devil, we must give the enemy no foothold. We must become strong persons who will not succumb to the enemy's attacks. We need to put on spiritual armor.

> Finally, be strong in the Lord and in the strength of
> his might. Put on the whole armor of God, that you
> may be able to stand against the wiles of the devil.
> For we are not contending against flesh and blood,
> but against the principalities, against the powers,
> against the world rulers of this present darkness,
> against the spiritual hosts of wickedness in the
> heavenly places. Therefore take the whole armor of
> God, that you may be able to withstand in the evil
> day and, having done all, to stand. Stand therefore,
> having girded your loins with truth, and having put
> on the breastplate of righteousness, and having shod
> your feet with the equipment of the gospel of peace;
> besides all these, taking the shield of faith, with which
> you can quench all the flaming darts of the evil one.
> And take the helmet of salvation, and the sword of
> the Spirit, which is the word of God. Pray at all times
> in the Spirit, with all prayer and supplication (Eph.
> 6:10-18).

Putting on the "breastplate of righteousness" refers to living according to the commands of God. It involves an act of the will and perseverance. Taking the "shield of faith" implies a constant assent to all that God has revealed and to his love for us, and it implies our trust and reliance on God in this battle. By taking the "helmet of salvation," we claim the effects of salvation that we have received through the blood of Christ. The "sword of the Spirit" is both Scripture and Jesus himself. We need to identify closely with Jesus, who is also our defender in this battle. We are not powerless in our struggles. We have a whole spiritual arsenal at our disposal.

We need faith and absolute trust in God. We can rely on his help to defeat the enemy. Since the devil is the father of lies, it is important that we love the truth. If we live in the light of Christ and do not deceive ourselves or others, the enemy will be less able to deceive us. We must live righteously and renounce all that evil spirits offer. Sin can provide the enemy with a point of contact and an entry into our lives.

> Be angry but do not sin; do not let the sun go down
> on your anger, and give no opportunity to the devil
> (Eph. 4:26-27).

We need to be alert. We need to resist the enemy.

> Be sober, be watchful. Your adversary the devil
> prowls around like a roaring lion, seeking someone to
> devour. Resist him, firm in your faith (1 Pet. 5:8-9).

> Resist the devil and he will flee from you (Jas. 4:7).

What happens if the enemy already has a foothold? How do you go about breaking his influence?

It may be that the enemy has an ongoing influence on your life. This may be due to sin or some other cause. Let us suppose, for example, that through some traumatic experience in your childhood the enemy has had some success in trying to make you a fearful person. There are three steps you should take to become free of his influence.

1. *Use spiritual discernment* to detect the extent of the influence of an evil spirit and to identify the major thrust of his activity in your life. Discernment is a gift of the Holy Spirit that tells you what things are due to natural causes and what things come from evil spirits. You have some discernment as a consequence of being a

Christian. It is good, however, to search out mature Christians with tested gifts of discernment to help you.

2. *Reject the enemy* with the authority of a Christian believer. Jesus has given you the power to do this.

> The seventy returned with joy, saying, "Lord, even
> the demons are subject to us in your name!" And he
> said to them, "I saw Satan fall like lightning from
> heaven. Behold, I have given you authority to tread
> upon serpents and scorpions, and over all the power
> of the enemy; and nothing shall hurt you. Neverthe-
> less do not rejoice in this, that the spirits are subject to
> you; but rejoice that your names are written in
> heaven" (Lk. 10:17-20).

You may choose the following prayer or one similar to it to reject the enemy: "In the name of Jesus, I renounce you, evil spirit, and want no part of what you offer me. In the name of Jesus, I command you to leave."

3. *Work to correct the bad habits* and any other unfortunate consequences of the demonic influence. You may be delivered in an instant from the influence of evil spirits, but you may need to work for some time on the accompanying weakness of character. Sinful habits must be changed and unsettled emotions must be redirected into proper channels. The enemy's sinful influence may be gone, but the weakness of the flesh must still be confronted.

Look at the positive side. Things are bound to get better. You will be freer to work on shortcomings once the enemy's efforts have been identified and thwarted. You can expect to make greater progress in virtue.

The support of other Christians can prove to be invaluable in our struggle with the enemy. The witness of others striving to live for Christ provides us with an encouraging environment for our own growth in the Lord. In a Christian community, we can stand fast with our brothers and sisters in solidarity against the work of the enemy, organizing to break his strongholds by the power of God, whether in our individual lives or in the influence of the world around us. Community can provide many mature gifts of the Spirit, including the charism of discernment, which can provide a clear picture of what the enemy is up to.

Shoulder to shoulder with brothers and sisters in the Lord, we can wage spiritual warfare against the enemy. Our prayers will join together as we call upon the power of Jesus to defeat our enemy.

Discussion Questions

1. Have you ever experienced anything that convinced you the devil exists? Can he affect you? How?

2. Read 2 Peter 2:11 and John 14:30. Why is the devil so powerful? How is his power limited?

3. Read 1 Corinthians 10:13 and James 4:7. Why is submission to God's will a sure way to overcome the power of the devil? Why can we be sure God will not allow us to be tempted beyond our strength?

4. How should Christians react to the current faddishness of Satanism and the occult? Why is involvement with the occult particularly dangerous?

5. Read Ephesians 6:10-18. How does this passage show how dangerous the devil is? Discuss all the spiritual helps—the "armor of God"—we have available to fight against the devil.

6. Read Luke 10:17-20. Why do Christians have authority over demons? How should we exercise this authority? Should we pray for others so that they can be freed from demonic attack? For ourselves?

CHAPTER SEVEN:
REPENTANCE

Daily Scripture Readings

1. Read 1 John 1:8-10. Do you realize that you are a sinner? Do you realize that Jesus will forgive your sins if you confess them? Pray that you never try to hide your sinfulness from the forgiving Jesus.

2. Read Matthew 5:27-28. Consider that some sins can be committed in the mind. Realize that Jesus sees our hearts as well as our actions. Confess sins of the mind to Jesus also and accept his forgiveness.

3. Read Psalm 51. Contemplate the sincerity of the psalmist and his humble conviction that God will forgive him despite the enormity of his sin.

4. Read 1 Corinthians 4:3-5. Should we judge others? Should we be concerned if others judge us? Can we keep anything hidden from the Lord?

5. Read Ephesians 2:1-10. Who brings life to people? How does God raise us up with Jesus? Are we saved by faith or by works?

6. Read 1 John 2:1-6. If we do commit sin, why can we consider Jesus our advocate? Note that the proof of our love for Jesus is that we live a righteous life.

7. Read Matthew 5:23-24. Is it enough to be reconciled with God or must we also be reconciled with persons we have offended? Which is easier? Why is it often so difficult to be reconciled with another person?

We have intellects and free wills. We are responsible for our actions. If we sin, we need to repent and seek reconciliation.

The world, the flesh and the devil can *influence* us toward sin and wrongdoing, but we are not helpless puppets. We have intellects and free wills. We can examine a situation and freely choose courses of action. We are personally responsible for what we do and for the consequences of our actions.

Our wrongdoing and sin have negative consequences for ourselves and for those around us. Through wrongdoing and sin, we do damage to ourselves and to our relationships. It becomes harder to do what is right.

Suppose I have a hot temper. I get angry one day and lash out at fellow workers. This can have a ripple effect. I may cause some of the workers to get angry at me and develop feelings of resentment. After I cool off, the anger I stirred up in my fellow workers may very well continue to grow. I may have contributed greatly to making the office an unfriendly place to work.

The more often I lose my temper, the harder it will be to keep control of my emotions and develop the virtue of patience. Each sinful act makes it easier for me to commit the next sinful act and harder to change my ways.

There is a difference between wrongdoing and sin. Wrongdoing denotes the objective fact of something done wrong. It does not necessarily involve personal guilt.

We sin when we freely engage in wrongdoing, knowing that we are doing wrong. For an act to be a sin, we must know the action is wrong, yet still freely do it. Sin brings in the notion of guilt and personal culpability.

Sin may involve doing something wrong or it can involve our failing to do something we ought to do. There are sins of omission and commission. Wrongdoing and sin can be external acts or internal acts; they can involve deeds or thoughts. As a matter of fact, we can act correctly externally but still be sinning in our hearts.

You have heard that it was said, "You shall not
commit adultery." But I say to you that everyone

who looks at a woman lustfully has already committed adultery with her in his heart (Mt. 5:27-28).

Our whole selves, not just our external behavior, must be
involved in pleasing the Lord.

Create in me a clean heart, O God, and put a new and
right spirit within me. The sacrifice acceptable to God
is a broken spirit; a broken and contrite heart, O God,
thou wilt not despise (Ps. 51:10,17).

Wrongdoing and sin are objective matters. Whether or not we
act or think in conformity with God's will is a matter of fact. Sin is
sin. Fact is fact. Some people today, however, do not believe in
objective right and wrong. There is no God, they say, to set down
rules of right and wrong. Christians, on the other hand, declare that
some actions and thoughts are objectively wrong. They can rely on
the clear teaching of Scripture, on the teachings of Christian tradition, on the teachings of the churches, and on their own reasoning
and consciences, based on these other sources.

If we say we have no sin, we deceive ourselves, and
the truth is not in us. If we confess our sins, (God) is
faithful and just, and will forgive our sins and cleanse
us from all unrighteousness. If we say we have not
sinned, we make him a liar, and his word is not in us
(1 Jn. 1:8-10).

The one objective standard by which to judge if something is
wrongdoing or a sin is God's unchangeable will which has been
revealed to us. God's will can be known through Scripture, through
Christian tradition, through the teaching of the church. We can
know God's will through prayer, through the exercise of the gifts of
the Holy Spirit, through the counsel of mature Christians. We can
judge with reasonable accuracy—but not infallibly—about the
rightness or wrongness of our thoughts and actions. Only the Lord,
however, can ultimately judge us accurately.

But with me it is a very small thing that I should be
judged by you or by any human court. I do not even
judge myself. I am not aware of anything against
myself, but I am not thereby acquitted. It is the Lord
who judges me. Therefore do not pronounce judgment before the time, before the Lord comes, who will
bring to light the things now hidden in darkness and
will disclose the purposes of the heart. Then every

man will receive his commendation from God (1 Cor. 4:3-5).

When we do wrong, we need to repent. We can be completely assured that the Lord is always waiting with open arms to forgive us.

When we do wrong, we have an obligation to admit our responsibility for our wrongdoing or sin and to repent.

> Unless you repent, you will all likewise perish (Lk. 13:3).

> Repent therefore of this wickedness of yours, and pray to the Lord that, if possible, the intent of your heart may be forgiven you (Acts 8:22).

The word for "repentance" in New Testament Greek is "*metanoia*," which means "to have another mind" or "to change one's mind." Thus, repentance is changing the wrong attitude of our hearts. Repentance produces a change in our behavior and brings our wills back into proper submission to God.

Repentance involves taking certain specific actions:

Being honest: I did this and it was wrong;

Feeling remorse: I am sorry that I did it;

Seeking reconciliation: I ask and receive forgiveness from the Lord and from the persons I have wronged;

Making reparation: I decide to repair the damage done by my sin or wrongdoing.

We should not omit to ask the Lord to forgive us. Later on in this chapter, we will consider how we are to ask forgiveness of the persons we may have hurt or offended. Here we need to stress the importance of making an explicit prayer something like this: "Jesus, I need your forgiveness. Please forgive me my sin."

We know the Lord is eager to forgive us, but we need to ask for his forgiveness. The jury is not out deliberating our case. There is no suspense about the verdict. The Lord's intention is to forgive us.

> If we confess our sins, he is faithful and just, and will forgive our sins and cleanse us from all unrighteousness (1 Jn. 1:9).

Jesus loved us while we were still sinners.

> But God, who is rich in mercy, out of the great love with which he loved us, even when we were dead

through our trespasses, made us alive together with
Christ (Eph. 2:4-5).

God sent his only Son to die for us.

For God so loved the world that he gave his only Son,
that whoever believes in him should not perish but
have eternal life. For God sent the Son into the world,
not to condemn the world, but that the world might
be saved through him (Jn. 3:16-17).

Jesus intercedes for us unceasingly before the throne of the
Father.

Is it Christ Jesus, who died, yes, who was raised from
the dead, who is at the right hand of God, who indeed
intercedes for us? (Rom. 8:34).

My little children, I am writing this to you so that you
may not sin; but if anyone does sin, we have an
advocate with the Father, Jesus Christ the righteous;
and he is the expiation for our sins, and not for ours
only but also for the sins of the whole world (1 Jn. 2:1-
2).

Jesus has opened up heaven to us.

Therefore, brethren, since we have confidence to enter
the sanctuary by the blood of Jesus, by the new and
living way which he opened for us through the
curtain, that is, through his flesh, and since we have a
great priest over the house of God, let us draw near
with a true heart in full assurance of faith, with our
hearts sprinkled clean from an evil conscience and
our bodies washed with pure water (Heb. 10:19-22).

These texts can give a great deal of confidence to anyone who
has doubts about God's mercy and forgiveness.

Christian churches and communities can support us in seeking
forgiveness from the Lord. Some churches have altar calls for those
persons seeking to repent of their sins and to turn their lives over to
the Lord. Sometimes quiet prayer support is offered to the penitent
sinner. Some churches have sacramental forms of reconciliation.

**We are responsible for the consequences of our wrong ac-
tions. We need to repair the damage we have caused.**

Actions have consequences. Wrong actions have consequences for which we are responsible. As best we can, we need to make things right again.

> If one member suffers, all suffer together (1 Cor.
> 12:26).

A hot temper can cause a lot of hurt feelings and resentment. Once we cool off, we must try and repair any damaged relationships. Often, of course, this is very hard to do.

Sins against justice need special care to see that reparation is done. If we defraud or steal from someone, we need to return the money or object taken. If a sales manager encourages his sales staff to act unjustly, he is responsible to see that the customers get their money back or get fair treatment. He also needs to see that his company regains its reputation for honesty.

Sinning is not nice. Sinning has all sorts of bad consequences. The repentant sinner has to do everything in his or her power to repair any damages caused.

> Be angry but do not sin; do not let the sun go down
> on your anger (Eph. 4:26).

> So if you are offering your gift at the altar and there
> remember that your brother has something against
> you, leave your gift there before the altar and go; first
> be reconciled to your brother and then come and offer
> your gift (Mt. 5:23-24).

Repentance for wrongdoing involves both seeking forgiveness and repairing the wrong. To be forgiven, we not only have to ask the Lord's forgiveness, but, if possible, the forgiveness of those whom we wronged. This forgiveness is more than the soothing of hurt feelings. We are in the debt of those we wronged. When they forgive us, they tear up this debt.

How do you ask for forgiveness from someone? You don't just look up at the ceiling or down at your shoes. You don't just hem and haw. You don't just give a vapid smile and make an inconsequential comment. You go up to the person, make eye contact and say: "What I did was wrong. Please forgive me." Note that you are asking for forgiveness for objective wrongdoing, not for some bad feelings you might have about the person.

It is not easy to ask for forgiveness. Sometimes it seems to be the most difficult thing you'll ever be called on to do. Still, you must do it. It often leads to a remarkable improvement in relationships.

There are four elements in asking for forgiveness.

1. There must be *an admission of wrongdoing* with no excuses. Don't blame your wrongdoing on problems in your childhood or on a lingering hangover. If you did wrong, admit it.

2. There must be a *genuine expression of remorse* along with an intention to change. Talk to the person face to face. Tell the person you are sorry and that you intend to change your behavior. It doesn't make much sense to ask for forgiveness unless you really intend to stop the bad behavior and do better in the future.

3. Acknowledge that the other party's forgiveness is *something to be asked for.* In other words, wait for the other person to respond.

4. Whenever possible, you *should actually repair the damage done by the wrongdoing.* Restore the other party's good name if you are guilty of slander. Repay any money taken unjustly or repair any damage to property. Work at healing any wounded relationships.

We have been talking about asking for forgiveness when there has been wrongdoing on our part. These principles can be adapted to a situation where there are damaged relationships because of an accident or misunderstanding and not because of real wrongdoing. We still need to do our best to repair damaged relationships even though there is no wrongdoing on our part.

What should we do if the other person does not forgive us? We need to be sensitive to the person's feelings. He or she has been hurt. We can ask ourselves if we have done everything we can to ask for forgiveness in the right way and to repair the wrong. The person may simply need more time to consider our apology. The person may seem confused and unable to respond when we say something like, "Do you forgive me?" If this approach to getting reconciled is so foreign to the person, we will have to find a less direct way of doing it. If the person simply refuses to grant forgiveness, then we might try harder to repair the wrongdoing by, for example, repeated acts of kindness.

On the other side of the coin, we should be ready to grant forgiveness. If the person asking to be forgiven is sincere, we should grant the forgiveness even though there may be some lingering hurt feelings. Forgiving is an act of the will. Our resentments do not automatically disappear when we exercise an act of the will. What we are deciding is that we will not hold this wrongdoing against the person any longer.

When someone asks for our forgiveness, the correct response is something like, "I forgive you." If there was wrongdoing involved, we should not pass this over by saying: "Oh, it was nothing." It *was* wrong, and it needs to be forgiven so the damaged relationship can be repaired.

Our wrong actions have their effect on us as well as on others. The more often we cheat someone, the more liable we are to cheat again. We need to work on building up our virtues of honesty and generosity, and ask the Lord to help us every day.

Discussion Questions

1. Read 1 John 1:8-10. How do we know if an act is objectively sinful? How do our intellects and wills enter into the act of sinning? What is a sin of omission? Give examples.

2. Define repentance. Discuss how repentance involves these specific actions of the intellect and will: honesty, remorse, reconciliation, reparation.

3. Read Ephesians 2:4-5 and John 3:16-17. Why can we be sure that God will forgive our sins? Why is it important that we ask Jesus specifically for forgiveness?

4. Read Romans 8:34 and 1 John 2:1-2. Discuss how Jesus is our special intercessor with the Father. Why is Jesus particularly effective at this?

5. Read 1 Corinthians 12:26 and Matthew 5:23-24. Discuss how our personal sin can affect the whole body of Christ. Why is it so important to be reconciled with our Christian brothers and sisters?

6. Discuss the four elements in asking for forgiveness: admission of wrongdoing, genuine expression of remorse, acknowledging the importance of forgiveness and repairing the wrongdoing.

Section Three

CHAPTER EIGHT: EVANGELIZING OTHERS

Daily Scripture Readings

1. Read Mark 16:15-20. Listen to the Lord's command to preach the gospel. Promise that you will obey his command. Think of the power with which the apostles spread the good news and claim that power for yourself.

2. Read Romans 10:13-17. How are people to learn about Jesus unless Christians tell them? Know that you are being asked by Jesus to share your faith. Have confidence that he will give you the strength to do this.

3. Read John 15:1-11. Think of the joy of being joined to Jesus as a branch is joined to the vine. Think of the sorrow you would experience if you were cut off from the vine. Now think of the many people who are not connected to the vine, Jesus. What can you do to help them become part of the body of Christ?

4. Read Acts 1:1-8. Consider that Jesus was establishing a heavenly kingdom, not an earthly one. Note that the apostles were not to go to the ends of the earth as witnesses on their own power. They were to wait until they were empowered through baptism in the Holy Spirit.

5. Read Matthew 10:24-33. If people criticize us because we follow the Lord, is that not a sign that we are doing something right? Consider humiliation and criticism as opportunities to share in the humiliation Jesus experienced. How will we respond on the judg-

ment day if Jesus asks us if we have acknowledged him before others?

6. Read 1 Corinthians 4:8-13. Which category do you fall into? Are you the honored, complacent believer or are you the hard-working, reviled apostle? Is God pleased with your efforts to spread his kingdom?

7. Read Luke 12:16-21. Are we laying up treasures in heaven? If so, then we are very wise. What about our neighbors? Are they only amassing earthly treasures? Shouldn't we tell them that these treasures will not last?

Evangelization is not optional. Jesus commands every Christian to be a witness. The Holy Spirit empowers us and compels us to spread the good news of salvation.

We should approach the topic of evangelization with joy. It is really exciting to lead someone to Christ or to lead someone to a closer walk with the Lord. Of course, we don't succeed every time we try.

My wife and I were baptized in the Spirit in June, 1974. We were bursting with enthusiasm and wanted to share this excitement with our friends. However, following the advice of the leaders of the prayer group, we decided to go slowly when witnessing about the charismatic renewal. That was good advice. Our friends who were not charismatics were quite leery about baptism in the Spirit.

Our best friends, another couple in the San Francisco Bay area, were also very cautious about the renewal. My wife and I wondered how we could talk about it without turning them off. Then a breakthrough came.

Our friends invited us over for dinner because they wanted us to talk about the charismatic renewal. ("Praise the Lord!," my wife and I said to each other privately.) Another couple, related to our best friends, had met some charismatics and wanted to learn more about the renewal. We were prepared to talk at great length about it, knowing that our friends would be listening, too.

The other couple was visiting from the Sacramento area. They recounted an interesting tale. Some of their friends had become involved in the charismatic renewal and this couple attended some of the gatherings of the charismatics. One of these occasions was a Thanksgiving dinner.

The charismatics got so wrapped up in praising God and fellowshipping that the host couple forgot to turn the oven on for the turkey. According to the story, they turned on the oven and prayed over the bird and an hour later it was all cooked. (It was not clear if the couple we were talking to actually witnessed the fast-cooking-bird incident or only heard about it.)

My wife and I used this story as an excuse to launch into an unreservedly enthusiastic panegyric about the unquestioned marvels of modern pentecostalism. We tripped over each other's tales in witnessing how the Lord had done such marvelous things to both of us. Then we both got the message at the same time and our torrent of words slowed to a trickle. This visiting couple were not looking for encouragement to get involved in the charismatic renewal. They were looking for some "sane" Christians to come up with a rational explanation for the "crazy" behavior of the charismatics in Sacramento. My wife and I were just as "crazy" as they were!

As far as I know, we made not the slightest positive impression on the couple from Sacramento. Though we remained close friends with the Bay Area couple, they have never become interested in the charismatic renewal. On the other hand, we have often shared religious values and insights and I think we may have encouraged them in their particular walk with the Lord.

I have read a number of dramatic conversion stories. One Christian man was sitting on a plane when he happened to look at a man across the aisle. He seemed to see the word "Adultery" on the man's forehead. He started talking to the man and, by the end of the flight, the man had turned away from the adulterous affair he was involved in.

Another Christian told about being moved by the Lord to stop and pick up a teenage hitchhiker. The man did not want to do it because it was raining and the teenager would get his car seats wet. Yet he did and discovered that the young man was about to commit suicide. He witnessed to him and the teenager accepted Jesus and returned to his family a few days later. He had run away from home.

I wish I had a real catchy story like these about my personal success in witnessing, but I don't. I've talked to a fair number of people about Jesus and I have seen some modest success in some instances, but nothing dramatic. I am the managing editor of a magazine dedicated to evangelization, *A.D. 2000 Together,* so I'm sure I'm helping spread the kingdom of the Lord that way. I have nothing very dramatic to share yet.

These final two chapters will give some tips on evangelizing that should be helpful to all Christians. In a special way, however, I hope those newly baptized in the Spirit will take the thoughts to heart. You have a special new-in-the-Spirit enthusiasm that can be very effective in the spread of the kingdom.

Most of us will not be called to be missionaries or street preachers, but all Christians are challenged to tell their friends and acquaintances about Jesus.

The Scriptures are quite clear about the obligation of all Christians to evangelize.

> And he said to them, "Go into all the world and preach the gospel to the whole creation. He who believes and is baptized will be saved, but he who does not believe will be condemned. And these signs will accompany those who believe: in my name they will cast out demons; they will speak in new tongues; they will pick up serpents, and if they drink any deadly thing, it will not hurt them; they will lay their hands on the sick, and they will recover." So then the Lord Jesus, after he had spoken to them, was taken up into heaven, and sat down at the right hand of God. And they went forth and preached everywhere, while the Lord worked with them and confirmed the message by the signs that attended it (Mk. 16:15-20).

> But how are men to call upon him in whom they have not believed? And how are they to believe in him of whom they have never heard? And how are they to hear without a preacher? And how can men preach unless they are sent? As it is written, "How beautiful are the feet of those who preach good news." But they have not all obeyed the gospel; for Isaiah says, "Lord, who has believed what he has heard from us?" So faith comes from what is heard, and what is heard comes by the preaching of Christ (Rom. 10:14-17).

These passages can make us feel inadequate. How can we go to a strange land to preach about Jesus? Will miraculous signs accompany our ministry? Will we have the power to cast out demons and to heal the sick? How can we know God's will for us?

The first two chapters of the Acts of the Apostles can help answer these questions.

Just before his ascension into heaven, Jesus tells his apostles: "You shall be my witnesses in Jerusalem and in all Judea and Samaria and to the end of the earth" (Acts 1:8). Yet what happened afterward? The apostles were cowering behind locked doors. They were afraid of being killed. They also were thinking of going back to Galilee and returning to former careers as fishermen. They weren't preaching to anybody where they were, much less making plans for missionary journeys to the end of the earth.

The first part of that verse, Acts 1:8, has the key. "You shall receive power when the Holy Spirit has come upon you." Acts 2 tells what does happen that first Pentecost. The Holy Spirit comes upon them in tongues of fire and they are changed. They start preaching to the crowds and 3,000 are baptized that first day. The coming of the Holy Spirit makes all the difference.

Keep your spirits up as you continue reading. The Holy Spirit will supply all the power you need for evangelization. Open your hearts. Approach the subject of evangelization with joy and enthusiasm. You don't have to rely on your own power. Rely on the Holy Spirit.

This chapter looks at why we should evangelize and how we can prepare ourselves to evangelize. The next chapter will consider the basic truths of the gospel and how we can bring those we evangelize to understand and accept these truths. In essence, we tell our friends and acquaintances how the Lord has touched us and changed us. People who know us and love us will be inclined to listen to us and care about the things that we care about. They can hear the gospel from someone they trust.

> But we were gentle among you, like a nurse taking care of her children. So, being affectionately desirous of you, we were ready to share with you not only the gospel of God but also our own selves, because you had become very dear to us (1 Th. 2:7-8).

> For though I am free from all men, I have made myself a slave to all, that I might win the more. To the weak I became weak, that I might win the weak. I have become all things to all men, that I might by all means save some. I do it all for the sake of the gospel, that I may share in its blessings (1 Cor. 9:19, 22-23).

Evangelizing others takes time, thought, effort and, above all, love.

Evangelization is a matter of salvation. It is a matter of heaven and hell. It is a matter of giving someone a most precious gift—the saving knowledge of Jesus Christ.

In regard to evangelization, evangelicals and Pentecostals consider the matter somewhat differently than Roman Catholics and mainline Protestants do. Looking at these differences can help us better understand the importance of evangelization.

Generally speaking, most evangelicals and Pentecostals consider the born-again experience or the baptism in the Spirit to be a matter of spiritual life and death. Before the individual accepts Jesus Christ as Lord and Savior, there is no salvation. The individual is destined for hell-fire. At the moment of the acceptance of Jesus as Lord and Savior, however, the individual becomes a Christian and receives the grace of justification. The Holy Spirit comes and begins to dwell within the person. Evangelization is of the utmost importance. Eternity depends on it.

Most Roman Catholics and mainline Protestants, on the other hand, believe there is salvation before the born-again or baptized in the Spirit experience. Babies are baptized and, among the sacramental churches, some other sacraments are bestowed on infants and children. A baptized baby is considered to be a Christian and belongs to the family of God. They believe that the graces of justification and the indwelling of the Holy Trinity come at baptism, which is usually infant baptism.

Roman Catholics and mainline Protestants also say that it is important for the adult Christian to accept the graces received as an infant and to come to the point of a personal decision for Christ. They consider it very important for every Christian to come into a genuine personal knowledge of Jesus Christ and to experience growth and life in the Holy Spirit. Salvation and some spiritual growth are possible without an explicit acceptance of Jesus as Lord and Savior, but the Christian life will be much more effective and alive through this acceptance and through baptism in the Spirit.

Catholics and Protestants also, in general, have a wider view of salvation. They see the possibility of good people who are not Christians being saved through the mercy and love of Jesus even though they don't know him. Sometimes this is called the "implicit baptism of desire." This teaching has a long history in the church.

In any case, evangelicals and Pentecostals and Protestants and Catholics all consider evangelization to be very important. People are to be evangelized so they will reject sin and accept Jesus as Lord and Savior. Water baptism is important. Growth in the spiritual life and the indwelling of the Holy Spirit are important. All Christians need to become very enthusiastic about evangelization.

We want to tell people about Jesus because we love them. When we evangelize, we grow spiritually.

Evangelizing is a matter of love. We love people and we want to see them get the very best. Knowing Jesus as Lord and Savior is the very best thing they can have.

For Jesus, evangelization is not something optional. He commands us to evangelize.

> And Jesus came and said to them, "All authority in heaven and on earth has been given to me. Go therefore and make disciples of all nations, baptizing them in the name of the Father and of the Son and of the Holy Spirit, teaching them to observe all that I have commanded you; and lo, I am with you always, to the close of the age" (Mt. 28:18-20).

We don't know the future. We don't know how many more years we will live. We don't know how long our friends have to live. If we don't effectively share the gospel with those we know, perhaps no one ever will. We can't be sure someone else will come along and witness to them. It could be a matter of our friends' eternal salvation, a matter of heaven or hell.

> For, "everyone who calls upon the name of the Lord will be saved." But how are men to call upon him in whom they have not believed? And how are they to believe in him of whom they have never heard? (Rom. 10:13-14).

With the infilling of the Holy Spirit, we have the power to evangelize effectively.

> But you shall receive power when the Holy Spirit has come upon you; and you shall be my witnesses in Jerusalem and in Judea and Samaria and to the end of the earth (Acts 1:8).

The Lord desires to give all men and women what he has given us.

> For God so loved the world that he gave his only Son,
> that whoever believes in him should not perish but
> have eternal life. For God sent the Son into the world,
> not to condemn the world, but that the world might
> be saved through him (Jn. 3:16-17).

Furthermore, if we don't share the gospel, we will dry up spiritually. When we share our faith, our faith comes alive. We need to pour out God's love to others in order to receive it more abundantly.

> I am the true vine, and my Father is the vinedresser.
> Every branch of mine that bears no fruit, he takes
> away, and every branch that does bear fruit, he
> prunes that it may bear more fruit (Jn. 15:1-2).

> So every one who acknowledges me before men, I
> also will acknowledge before my Father who is in
> heaven; but whoever denies me before men, I also
> will deny before my Father who is in heaven (Mt.
> 10:32-33).

It's not easy to evangelize. We can feel embarrassed. We can be fearful. Still, with the power of the Holy Spirit, we can overcome all obstacles to evangelization.

Maybe we lack fervor. Maybe we lack a strong love of God and a strong love of our brothers and sisters. If that is the case, we need to meditate on God's love for us and for all men and women. We can think of the cross, of the price our Lord paid for our salvation and their salvation.

> For God so loved the world that he gave his only Son
> (Jn. 3:16).

We can also think of the rejoicing in heaven over one repentant sinner.

> There is joy before the angels of God over one sinner
> who repents (Lk. 15:10).

Stories of missionaries or evangelizers can move us. Testimonies of how people came to be saved can convince us of the importance of evangelization. Personal testimonies can be moving. People who give their lives to Jesus or who are filled with the Holy Spirit can be eloquent in witnessing to the importance of evangelization.

It is one thing, however, to believe that God wants you to evangelize. It is quite another thing to go out and actually witness. We are so afraid of what other people will think about us if we share our faith.

In a sense, we have to be in sales. Now, there are many different types of salespersons. We don't have to go up and down the street ringing doorbells. We can share about Jesus in our own quiet way, but we must share. We have something so precious, Jesus, that we need to help others see how precious a treasure he is.

Here are some of the objections we may have to evangelizing.

I'm not holy enough. That is true, but God is holy enough. God will do the saving. God will give the gift of faith. We are just instruments in the process. We may be unworthy instruments, but we are necessary.

> I planted, Apollos watered, but God gave the growth
> (1 Cor. 3:6).

I don't know where to begin. This chapter and the next chapter can help. Start with friends and acquaintances. Pray for guidance.

I don't have the gift. I'm not an evangelist or public speaker. We are not talking in this chapter about the specific charismatic gift of evangelism. We are talking here about the basic responsibility all Christians have to evangelize. God has given you the power through his Spirit. (See Acts 1:8.) If God can speak through an ass (Num. 22:28-30), he can speak through you.

I'm embarrassed that I might be identified with those "evangelists." This is just vanity. Do you care more about what men and women think of you than what God thinks of you?

> So every one who acknowledges me before men, I
> also will acknowledge before my Father who is in
> heaven; but whoever denies me before men, I also
> will deny before my Father who is in heaven (Mt.
> 10:32-33).

I won't succeed. I'll look foolish. This is another form of vanity. Even though we may be rejected when we witness, we may have planted a seed that another Christian will reap the harvest of later.

We should be ready to seem to be fools for Christ.

> For I think that God has exhibited us apostles as last
> of all, like men sentenced to death; because we have
> become a spectacle to the world, to angels and to
> men. We are fools for Christ's sake, but you are wise
> in Christ. We are weak, but you are strong. You are
> held in honor, but we are in disrepute (1 Cor. 4:9-10).

I might get laughed at or persecuted. Persecution in this case is a sign that you are doing something right. You are pricking the consciences of people.

> Blessed are you when men revile you and persecute
> you and utter all kinds of evil against you falsely on
> my account. Rejoice and be glad, for your reward is
> great in heaven, for so men persecuted the prophets
> who were before you (Mt. 5:11-12).

I can't impose my beliefs on others. We're not talking about your opinions; we're talking about eternal truths. All people face an eternity of either heaven or hell. God's love and forgiveness are available for all people. They must be told about these things.

They seem happy enough where they are. Earthly happiness is fleeting. It will pass. Also, the appearance of happiness may disguise a really bad situation. Lasting happiness in this life and in eternity only comes through a relationship with Jesus.

> And he told them a parable, saying, "The land of a
> rich man brought forth plentifully; and he thought to
> himself, What shall I do, for I have nowhere to store
> my crops? And he said, 'I will do this: I will pull
> down my barns, and build larger ones; and there I
> will store all my grain and my goods. And I will say
> to my soul, Soul, you have ample goods laid up for
> many years; take your ease, eat, drink, be merry.' But
> God said to him, 'Fool! This night your soul is re-
> quired of you; and the things you have prepared,
> whose will they be?' So is he who lays up treasure for
> himself and is not rich toward God" (Lk. 12:16-21).

How do we begin evangelizing? Whom should we approach first? What do we say?

We can't share what we don't have. We need to grow in

knowledge and love of the Lord. We need to pray daily and let the Lord develop our relationship with him. We need to become very familiar with the Bible. (You may want to review Chapters One and Two of this book.)

Perhaps we can get a leaflet with some basic principles or some basic Bible texts that we can share with the person. Some Christians have found it helpful to study the Gospel of Mark carefully. It's the shortest and in some ways the clearest of the Gospels. We can practice explaining it to others.

We don't need to worry about understanding abstruse theological arguments. We can just share what the Lord has done for us. We can tell people how we have changed. Nobody can argue with that.

Whom do we talk to? As a rule, we start with those closest to us. We have relationships with many people already and we can deepen relationships with persons we want to witness to. We can start evangelizing our family, our friends and those we come in contact with at work or at church. People who know us and love us will listen to us.

We might even want to write out a list of people with whom we have relationships. We can pray over this list and ask the Lord for discernment about where to begin. The easiest person to talk to might not be the one the Lord would have us contact first. Maybe we should talk with the greatest sinner among our acquaintances.

Once we have decided which persons among our acquaintances we should approach first, we need to pray specifically for them and for our witnessing to them. We should make sure our relationships with them are strong. We may need to spend some extra time with them to rebuild our friendship.

Then we need to go for it. We need to take the plunge. We need to talk with them about the Lord. We'll say more about this in the next chapter.

Discussion Questions

1. Read Mark 16:15-20. Why does every Christian have the obligation to evangelize? What does Jesus say about salvation and damnation? What signs accompany those preaching the gospel? Do these signs occur today?

2. Read Romans 10:14-17. How can a person accept Jesus as

Lord and Savior unless the person hears of Jesus? If we have the opportunity to witness about Jesus and do not witness, do we have assurances that another Christian will witness to the person? If the person is condemned to hell, are we somewhat guilty if we have neglected an opportunity to evangelize the person?

3. What should we do about lukewarm Christians we know? Should we encourage them to become more effective Christians? Should we "leave it to God"?

4. Read Matthew 10:32-33. Do you think Jesus is serious about this? Imagine yourself before the judgment seat of God, forced to admit that because of embarrassment you never told anyone about Jesus. What do you think Jesus will say to you?

5. Discuss some of the common excuses to avoid evangelizing: I'm not holy enough; I don't have the gift; I'm embarrassed; I might get persecuted; they seem happy enough the way they are.

6. Think of the people you can witness to. How should you begin? How do you bring up the subject of Jesus? Will they reject you if you do?

CHAPTER NINE:
PERSONAL TESTIMONY

Daily Scripture Readings

This week, as we prepare to consider the power of personal testimony, we will meditate on some episodes from the Acts of the Apostles.

1. Read Acts 1:15-26. Consider the despair of Judas and his lack of repentance. Realize that Jesus was eager to forgive Judas if only he had asked for forgiveness. Consider the selection of Matthias to be an apostle. Are you following the call God has given you?

2. Read Acts 2:1-13. Consider how the power of the Holy Spirit profoundly changed those in the upper room. Think of the way the city reacted. How can you use the power of the Spirit to change your city?

3. Read Acts 3:1-10. Marvel at the healing power manifested through Peter and John. Know that Jesus continues to heal today. Are you praying with confidence for healing?

4. Read Acts 5:1-11. Ananias and Sapphira were very generous, but they were not completely honest. Meditate on the purity of heart required of the true follower of Jesus.

5. Read Acts 9:1-19. Continue to pray for the conversion of people you know, no matter how hopeless the case may seem to be. God can overcome all obstacles.

6. Read Acts 12:1-17. As God delivered Peter from prison, so he can deliver us from our difficulties, no matter how serious they are. Continue to pray for help and trust in the Lord and step out in faith when help arrives.

7. Read Acts 13:1-12. Honor leaders who have been set aside for the work of the Lord. Pray for discernment to recognize false teachers.

You don't need to be a preacher or a Scripture scholar to witness about the Lord. Just give your personal testimony. Tell others about the way Jesus saved you and changed your life.

I was blessed by being born into a loving Christian family. My mother died in childbirth, but my grandmother raised me with great affection and tenderness. I was baptized as an infant and received other Catholic sacraments at appropriate ages. I went to Catholic schools. I remained a devout Catholic through college and years of teaching in Catholic schools.

When I was 36, I left teaching in California to pursue a newspaper career in Iowa and back in California. This career change coincided with sort of a religious burnout. I continued to attend Mass on Sunday, but that was about it. I rarely prayed. I did not feel any sort of a personal relationship with the Lord. I kept up an academic interest in religion, however, and subscribed to several religious publications.

As I look back on that time, I now can see the hand of the Lord protecting me from getting into any real serious difficulties. My innocence and naivete also protected me. My apartment complex in the San Francisco Bay area, I found out later, was a swinging singles' place, but I didn't know it at the time. I married a good Christian woman.

I was working on the copy desk of the *Oakland Tribune* when the religion writer died, and I applied for and got the job. I thoroughly enjoyed covering religion stories and lots of wild things were happening in the Bay Area religion scene. A priest friend tried several times to get me to write a story about Catholic charismatics. I had researched and written stories about religious social action and seminaries and active parishes and gurus and cults and anticult organizations, but I sure didn't want to write about charismatics. The priest friend persisted and I finally wrote a story about a Catholic priest active in the renewal. I was favorably impressed and the story reflected my positive attitude.

A week or so later, I got a call from a local Assemblies of God pastor. My first thought was that he was going to complain about something, but the pastor, Paul Schoch, surprised me by praising my story about the charismatic priest. He went on to say that he was cosponsor of an upcoming interdenominational charismatic conference and he offered to set up some people to interview if I wanted to do a story. I made an appointment to come to his church.

When driving over to his church, which was not too far from the downtown office of the *Oakland Tribune,* I had a very strong urge to turn around and go back to the office. I had been to many cult headquarters and other unusual places for stories, but here I was, hesitating about going to an established Pentecostal church. I didn't turn back, however.

Paul Schoch turned out to be a large, cheerful man. There was a small man with him, the other cosponsor of the conference. This was the first time I had met David du Plessis, a leading figure in the worldwide Pentecostal/charismatic renewal movement. I interviewed both of them and wrote a favorable article.

The next year, I wrote at least a half dozen articles on charismatics. I came to look forward to doing a story on them because their faith was so vibrant. I even said to myself once or twice that I ought to go to a prayer meeting.

The next year, Pastor Schoch set up an interview for me with three speakers at the charismatic conference that year. I went to his church and got the story and then one of the speakers, another Assemblies of God pastor, complimented me on the stories I had written and asked me if I was filled with the Holy Spirit. I said I wasn't, at least in the sense they talked about. He looked me in the eye and asked: "Can we pray over you?"

I was petrified. I wasn't ready for this. I had heard about the dramatic changes that take place when you let the Holy Spirit in. I didn't know what to do. Then Paul Schoch came to my rescue. "Can we pray over you for your ministry?," he asked. I knew my writing could use all the help it could get, so I agreed and they prayed over me.

About four months later, I started going to prayer meetings and I liked them. I told one of the prayer-group leaders about my being prayed over a few months before. "It didn't take, though," I said, meaning that I had not been baptized in the Spirit at the time. "You're here, aren't you?," was all he said and I realized that my

coming to the prayer meetings was somehow a result of being
prayed over. It occurred to me that they had played a trick on me
in Pastor Schoch's office. They prayed that I receive the Spirit,
knowing that the Spirit would do a lot more than simply help me
in my writing.

I was grateful that, in a sense, I had been tricked into coming
into a deeper relationship with the Lord. I was prayed over for
baptism in the Spirit about two months after starting to come to
prayer meetings. My life was changed instantaneously. I knew that
Jesus loved me. Scripture came alive for me. My personal prayer
life was much fuller. Prayer meetings and liturgies provided me a
clear sense of the presence of God. This spiritual vitality has
remained for more than 14 years and there do not seem to be any
signs of its diminishing.

This is my basic personal testimony of how I came to the Lord.
In this chapter, we'll help you develop your own personal testimony.

**Just tell your own story in your own words. Don't worry
about people putting you on the spot with tricky questions. You
know your story better than anybody else.**

People like stories. Jesus frequently spoke in parables. Some
of the most effective parts of sermons are stories. News magazines
and television news programs tell the news through individual
stories. People like to hear about other people.

You have something to tell. God has worked in your life in a
unique way. No one else has your testimony. Your story will be
believable because you're talking about what happened to you.
You'll be completely convincing because you know it happened
that way.

The most common fear about witnessing is that you will be
presented with complicated arguments that you cannot answer.
You are afraid they will throw one objection from Scripture after
another at you. Or you are afraid people will ask how a good God
can allow so much evil in the world or how a good God can
condemn someone to hell for all eternity for doing things which
may be accepted by society in general. You feel that you will get
twisted into knots if you try to answer every possible objection.

The solution is not to get involved in theological or philosophical debates. Tell your story. Tell how God saved you and gave

special meaning to your life. No one can refute you. It happened to you. Get the other person to admit that God has done wonders in your life. Tell the person that God can do wonders for that individual, too.

The theological and philosophical questions are often excuses for the person to avoid facing reality and developing a closer relationship with Jesus. Get the person to pray. Pray with the person. Accompany the person to a prayer meeting or meaningful church service. Encourage the reading of Scripture. For the complicated theological and philosophical questions, direct the person to a reliable Bible class or discussion group. A counseling session with a church leader could help. Good books can be recommended.

Do not be put off by questions and objections. Tell your experience of God's love. It is bound to have an impact. You can help the person move closer to the Lord.

It should be clear that you are witnessing for a purpose. You are not just talking to hear yourself talk. The Lord has done wonders in your life and this is too good to keep. You need to spread the good news. Your goal in sharing your testimony is to have the other person become open to the Lord acting in power.

When the person sees the gospel applied to your situation, he or she can better understand the gospel message. Your personal testimony makes the person well-disposed to faith.

People can see that their own situations are not unique or hopeless. You were like them in some respects and things worked out well for you. Your personal testimony gives them reason for hope. God's grace worked for you, it can work for them.

Tailor your testimony to the person you're witnessing to. Address the particular needs of that individual.

If the person you are talking to is one you know well, you can tailor your testimony to the person's needs. You might ask yourself the question: What is the next step this person needs to take to move closer to the Lord?

If you don't know the person well, you may want to take time to learn more about him or her before sharing your testimony. You may want to take time to build up a trusting relationship, too. If you are only nodding acquaintances, the person may very well be taken aback if you suddenly started sharing intimate details of your life.

Perhaps the person knows nothing about God. Your testimony needs to begin at the beginning. Talk about how important it is to realize that there is a Creator who has prepared a place of heavenly reward. Talk about the gift of faith.

Maybe the individual has a vague belief in God, but needs to come to know Jesus as a personal Savior. You may want to focus your testimony on the way the Gospels have come alive for you and how you feel the presence of Jesus in your life. Talk about your growing personal relationship with your Savior whom you trust completely. Talk about the mystery of this God who became man and suffered, died and rose from the dead.

Perhaps this individual is a practicing Christian who needs to experience the power to live a life dedicated to Jesus. You might want to describe how the baptism in the Spirit changed your life. Now you have the power of the Holy Spirit energizing your life. Now you can pray with fervor. Now you can read Scripture with understanding. Now you can relate to others with the love that Jesus has for them.

Know your personal testimony well. Reflect often on the way God worked in your life during your conversion and on the way he continues to work in your daily life. Be able to adapt your testimony so it will have the greatest impact on the people you are witnessing to.

Witnessing will only be really effective when the person is ready to listen. Many times a person is only ready to hear about Jesus when he or she is in trouble. It could be sickness or the death of a loved one or the loss of a job. Often then the person is willing to hear about the love of God and the powerful way God can act in one's life. When tragedy strikes someone, give the best gift you can—the saving knowledge of Jesus.

Good times can also provide an opportunity for you to witness. If the person is going to get married or just had a baby, the conversation can often be shifted to the discussion of life's important values. Serious talk about the meaning of life is not out of place, especially at these times. Insurance salesmen know that times of change, times of triumph and tragedy, are times that people are more open to talk about serious subjects. Perhaps the major religious holidays can also provide opportunities for sharing one's testimony. Witnessing can be much more effective if timed right.

Use good storytelling techniques. Your testimony should

have a beginning, a middle and an end.

Don't be afraid to use good storytelling techniques. Build up suspense. Arouse interest. Take your time. Ask questions. Seek responses.

Advance preparation is important, especially if you've never given your testimony before. Don't just plunge in blindly. Take time to reflect on the way the Lord has worked in your life. Pray about it. Pick out the key points. Then write out a three-minute testimony. Practice giving it. Share it with Christian friends and with church leaders. Accept advice about making it more effective.

The outline of your testimony should have three parts: the beginning, the middle and the end.

Beginning. Talk briefly about your life before you came to know the Lord. Talk about your general family background. Mention experiences you have in common with the person you're witnessing to. Show how your life at this time was not fulfilled.

Middle. How did you come to know the Lord? Who witnessed to you? Why did you accept Jesus as Lord? How did you overcome obstacles? Describe the actual decision to follow the Lord. What did you experience immediately afterward?

End. What has happened since you accepted the Lord? How did your relationship with God change? How did your relationship with the church change? How did your relationship with people change? Give specific examples.

Be natural. Be confident. Do not use jargon. Don't say such things as: "God told me"; "God laid it on my heart"; "I've been washed in the blood"; "This is my testimony." People who have never heard these and similar statements may very well be turned off by them.

Be realistic and honest. Avoid exaggerating. Don't be arrogant and pushy. At times, it might be beneficial to talk about the depths of degradation that God delivered us from, but we should never glamorize sin. Sin is never glamorous.

You can say to the other person that your willingness to share about Jesus is an example of your new maturity in the Lord. You can also quote some Scripture passages to illustrate your story.

The testimony I shared at the beginning of this chapter tells about the way I was led to seek baptism in the Spirit. It was the most powerful religious experience in my life. The second most powerful experience came about quite unexpectedly.

Our charismatic community had a short retreat during which we prayed for a special new outpouring of the Spirit. I didn't really expect anything. At best, I thought I might get some sort of a consolation in prayer.

What I got was an instantaneous understanding that God is my Father. I was moved to pray, "Abba, Father," and mean it very deeply and personally. I knew as completely as I could know anything that God loves me personally as his son with an infinite love. It was a splendid gift from God.

In explaining it later, I used this example. Suppose I was a little child again, and I died and went to the gates of heaven and there found three doors with these signs on them: "The Father," "The Son," "The Holy Spirit." I, as a little child, would certainly not go to the door marked "The Holy Spirit" because I did not know anything about the Holy Spirit. I definitely would not enter the door marked "The Father" because I would be too terrified to do so. I probably would try to muster as much courage as I could and slowly open the door marked "The Son."

Now, after this special blessing and insight, I would run with a great deal of love and fling open the door marked "The Father." I know I would be welcomed with complete love. I would also feel a childlike peace about the other two doors, but the one I would run to would be that of my Father.

Discussion Questions

1. Do you remember the stories people tell you about themselves? Why is personal testimony an effective way to evangelize? Are your friends and acquaintances interested when you share personal experiences? Do you share important things about yourself regularly? Never? Too often?

2. Why should you adapt your personal testimony to specific circumstances? Does every person you talk to have the same level of personal faith and commitment to the Lord? Do some people, as it were, need to be fed meat and others only milk?

3. It has been said that there are no atheists in foxholes. Why is a time of crisis a good time to witness? Share your experiences about how you acted in a time of crisis.

4. Discuss your testimony in terms of having a beginning, a

middle and an end. What key points should be included in the beginning, in the middle and at the end? What points should receive the most emphasis?

5. Give some examples of witnessing that turned you off. Give some examples of good and effective ways people witnessed to you.

6. Share your personal testimony with others in the discussion group.